Moisture-loving Plants

Moisture-loving Plants

Philip Swindells

WARD LOCK

First published in Great Britain in 1991
by Ward Lock Limited, Villiers House,
41/47 Strand, London WC2N 5JE, England
A Cassell Imprint
© Ward Lock Ltd

Text filmset in Formby
by Chapterhouse
Printed and bound in Portugal
by Resopal

British Library Cataloguing in Publication Data
Swindells, Philip
   Moisture-loving plants.
   1. Gardens. Water plants.
   I. Title   II. Series
   635.9674

ISBN 0 7063 6980 7

CONTENTS

ACKNOWLEDGEMENTS

The publishers are grateful to the following agencies for granting permission to reproduce the following colour photographs: Harry Smith Horticultural Photographic Collection (pp. 11, 47, 59); Pat Brindley (pp. 55, 83) and Photos Horticultural (p. 14).

All the line drawings were by Nils Solberg.

PREFACE

The great surge of interest in water gardening in recent years brought about by the introduction of pre-formed pools and pool liners has also increased interest and awareness of all the wonderful marginal, bog and moisture-loving plants that are available to us. You need not have a pond to have a bog garden either; such a feature is not difficult to contrive elsewhere in the garden. Stream and ditch banks are also suitable locations for many of these lovely plants. This book aims to show just how wide a range of suitable plants there is and describes how and where to grow them, even if you do not have a natural wet patch and only limited space available.

P.R.S.

CHAPTER 1

THE BOG GARDEN

A bog garden provides tremendous opportunities for the adventurous gardener to cultivate a wide range of colourful and interesting plants that are impossible to grow under ordinary garden conditions. Logically such a feature is attached to a pool. However, if you do not have room for a full-blown water garden there are still ample opportunities to create a bog garden alone.

THE BOG GARDEN AND POOL

If you intend to have a bog garden alongside a pool choose, if you can, to construct the pool using a pool liner for this will ensure a much better end result. It is also prudent to organize the construction of the bog garden at the same time, for while it is not impossible to create such a feature afterwards, it can be extremely awkward. If your pool is to be made from pre-formed fibreglass, any bog garden then has to be built completely separately anyway.

A pool liner is a sheet of heavy gauge rubber, PVC or polythene material which is used to line an excavation and is moulded to its contours to form a waterproof lining. The sheet should be large enough to line the garden pool and the shallow area adjacent which is to become the bog garden. Management of both features will then be much simpler, the water from the pool moistening the soil in the boggy area and plants from the bog tumbling into the pool and disguising the edge. To look effective, the bog garden should be of a similar surface area to the pool.

It is very important both with a pool and a bog garden to consider carefully the virtues of the various pool liners available. Both pool and bog garden construction is hard work and therefore first-quality materials are justified as much here, if not more than anywhere else, in the garden. If a difficulty arises with a liner of inadequate quality, correcting the problem will involve a lot more very hard work. So quality and adequacy of size are paramount.

POLYTHENE LINERS
The lower price range of pool liners is dominated by those made of 500-gauge polythene. These are adequate for an independent bog garden, but have considerable limitations when used for a garden pool. A pool and bog garden combination should never be contemplated with a polythene liner. Apart from

the greater difficulty of installation owing to its lack of elasticity, a polythene liner rapidly deteriorates in sunlight, particularly any area that is exposed above water level. This is often inevitable when a liner is used to extend a pool into a bog garden, for however cleverly contrived, some of the polythene will always be exposed until adequate plant growth can be made.

BUTYL AND PVC LINERS

Butyl rubber and PVC liners present no such problems. The rubber kind is the most durable, but also the most expensive. However, there are new PVC liners that have been well tried in industry and these are likely to become more widely available, presenting a significant challenge to the dominance of the rubber type. In the meantime, however, butyl rubber is the best option for it has greater elasticity and is easier to install. Its rougher texture is also attractive to the establishement of microflora. These become easily attached and within a few months colonize the liner surface and help to disguise it. PVC, on the other hand, is shiny and difficult for algae and similar minute plants to attach to, so it will take a year or so before its harsh appearance has been diminished.

MEASURING AND EXCAVATING

Once the type of liner to be used has been decided upon, it is then necessary to calculate the size. In addition to the amount required for the pool, it will be necessary to take into account an additional length that embraces the area of the base of the bog garden and accumulation of totals for the depths (the minimum being 30 cm (12 in) at any one point, preferably more). A generous allowance for an overlap is also necessary (Fig. 1).

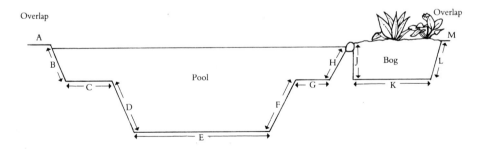

Fig. 1 Diagram showing how to calculate the amount of liner material needed in making a pool/bog garden. Depth J and L should be no less than 30 cm (1 ft), 45 cm (1½ ft) would be better. Distance $A + B + C + D + E + F + G + H + J + K + L + M =$ total liner length.

Primula rosea heralds the arrival of spring.

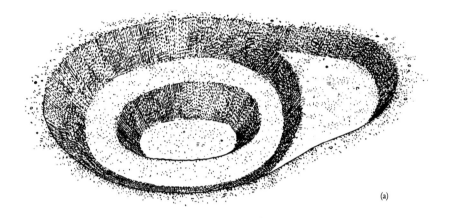

(a)

Fig.2 *Construction of composite pool and bog garden*
(a) Excavate the pool with an additional shallow area to provide a bog garden. For the best effect the bog area should be about one-third of the surface area of the adjacent pool.

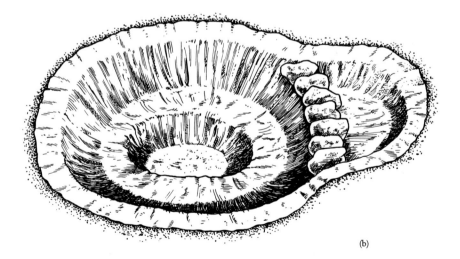

(b)

(b) Install the liner carefully, following the contours of the bog feature. The pool should be divided from the bog garden by a line of stones. These should not emerge higher than the surrounding ground.

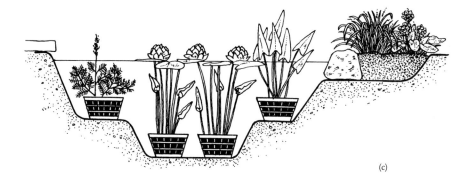

(c) The bog garden area should be filled with a suitable compost, using the stones to prevent it from slipping into the pool. Top dressing the area with pea shingle is an optional extra.

Both pool and bog garden should be dug out at the same time (Fig. 2*a*) the bog garden area being rather like a small spreading pool with a depth of between 30 and 45 cm (12–18 in). Take just as much care when lining the excavation for the bog garden as when dealing with the pool, for it is vital to have a watertight lining, especially on free-draining soils. Indeed, a leaking bog garden can considerably lower the water level of a connected pool in a warm summer spell.

As with a garden pool scour the excavation for sticks, stones or anything else that may puncture the liner. On gravelly soils, or on those where there may be flints, spread a generous layer of damp sand over the base of the excavation and smooth up the sides. Allow for this extra protective thickness when calculating the size of the excavation. Such a precaution is well worth taking and virtually eliminates any prospect of a puncture when the soil is replaced.

The dividing line between a bog garden and a pool should always be marked with a row of bricks or stones arranged in such a way that they do not offend the eye (Fig. 2*b*). It is this small retaining wall that keeps the soil of the bog garden out of the pool, but allows water to percolate through the soil and create boggy conditions. Ideally the soil surface should be 5 cm (2 in) above water level (Fig. 2*c*) The soil mixture that is replaced in the bog area can usually comprise the soil which has been removed, unless it is of a very sandy nature, in which case it should be mixed with a generous quantity of coarse peat or well-rotted garden compost or leaf mould.

Primula florindae, the Himalyan cowslip, lights up the waterside as summer slips away.

AN INDEPENDENT BOG GARDEN

A bog garden does not have to be attached to a pool to be successful. Some of the finest to be seen are completely independent entities in other parts of the garden. Providing that the situation is open and sunny, or no more than partly shaded, there is no reason at all why such a feature cannot be created. As it will not have water filtering into it from an adjacent pool, however, it is important that the site has ready access to a hosepipe, for in dry spells it is often necessary to raise the soil moisture level.

The independent bog garden can be constructed using a liner, broadly along the lines described previously. Alternatively it can be made of concrete or a pre-formed shallow pool sunk into the garden, but neither of these latter options is as easy to turn into a bog garden feature, either practically or aesthetically. While it is true to say that the expert in concrete construction can build an excellent structure in which to create a bog garden, the expertise of the professional cannot be easily transferred to the average weekend gardener, for whom attempting such an enterprise single-handed may court disaster.

A well-made bog garden using a pool liner should not present any serious problems for the home gardener or handyman. Construction follows along the lines described for the joint pool and bog garden except that, within reason, the deeper the bog excavation the better (Fig. 3). Certainly 45 cm (18 in) should be regarded as the minimum if the soil mixture is to remain moist throughout the summer. Shallow excavations lead to rapid drying out of the soil and all the attendant problems that this brings.

With a bog garden that stands alone a polythene liner can be used, for such a construction leaves no part of the liner exposed and at risk from damaging sun rays. It is slightly more tedious to install, for it has little flexibility, but it does make for an expensive construction, especially if, instead of a proprietary pool liner, heavy-gauge transparent builders' polythene is used. This is inexpensive and available off the roll in almost any size imaginable.

With both the combined pool and bog garden, and the free-standing bog, the finish at the edges is difficult to complete in a neat manner. There are many options open, but there are two which are simple and very effective. If the bog garden is to have a fairly straight, formal outline, then lengths of timber can be used and the edge of the liner wrapped around these and secured with wooden lathes. The wood and liner can then be placed just beneath the surface of the surrounding garden. It is even possible to turf up and over the edge. The liner protects the wood from rotting and the whole arrangement means that if alterations or major maintenance operations have to be conducted, finding and securing the edge of the lining is simple. If an informal outline is desired, bricks can be used as an alternative. This is a little more time-consuming to arrange, for

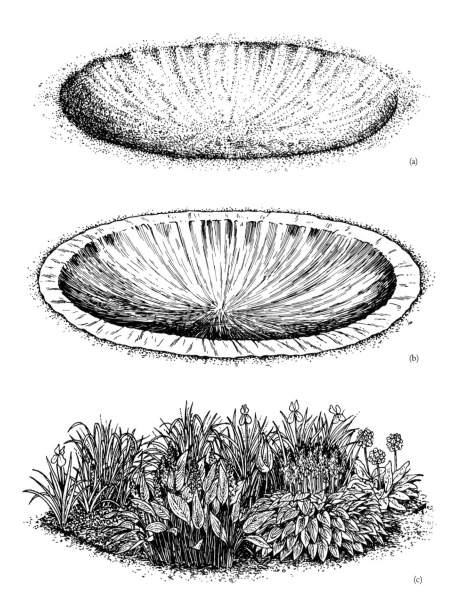

Fig. 3 *Construction of bog garden*
(a) Excavate the bog area to an even depth of 30–45 cm (12–18 in), and remove any sharp stones which could puncture the lining.
(b) Line the pool with a flexible liner, securing the top so that later it can be disguised.
(c) Fill with suitable moisture-retentive soil mixture, covering the overlap; water well and then plant. This stage shows the bog garden fully planted up.

each individual brick is wrapped in the edge of the liner and placed against the next. However, it allows great flexibility in making an informal edge.

The soil mixture should be the same for a free-standing bog as for the bog attached to a pool. Plenty of organic matter should be mixed in with the soil before replacement. If any fertilizer is to be added, it should be a slow-release kind, like bonemeal or hoof and horn. Indeed, throughout the life of the bog garden any regular applications of fertilizer should be of this kind, although a number of the modern foliar feeds can be used freely without presenting any problem. The soil moisture content should be constantly monitored in an independent bog garden, for in hot weather it can soon become very dry. Regular watering is essential, for although the liner prevents water escaping into the surrounding soil, most bog garden plants have quite expansive foliage which transpires freely.

CONVERTING A WET PATCH

The ideal wet area is one that has a regular uninterrupted water supply and has been well cultivated. Most gardeners are unlikely to have such a feature, for once a wet patch is cultivated it often dries out. However, if you do have a damp area in the garden it is well worth attempting to convert it into a bog garden for if it turns out to be a permanently wet place it will be the most perfect site for cultivating moisture-loving plants.

Most places of this kind are untamed when you come upon them and are likely to have been colonized by troublesome weeds like rushes and sedges. These will doubtless have been seeding themselves freely for some years and so once the adult plants are removed and the soil disturbed the seed bank in the soil will come to life and masses of undesirable seedlings will appear. Weed cover is not easy to remove either, for most native marsh plants are either tussock-forming or deep-rooted, or both. This makes their removal with a minimum of soil very difficult. Herbicides can be used very successfully, but the most efficient kinds take a long time to complete their task and so plenty of thought should go into planning well ahead.

Many wetland plants have glossy waxy waterproof foliage which does not readily accept water-based herbicides. A sticking agent, such as washing-up liquid or, in the case of troublesome weeds like mare's tail, an additive to break down the protective waxy coating of the foliage, is essential. Adding 25% by volume of household paraffin to a pre-mixed systemic herbicide containing glyphosate usually ensures that the foliage of weeds such as mare's tail readily accepts the herbicide.

Careful consideration must always be given to the application of herbicides on wet land, especially if the dampness of the soil is associated with a water course or other aquatic feature. Residual herbicides can cause immense environmental damage in wet areas and should never be contemplated, especially when planting has to be undertaken soon after clearance. Systemic herbicides in which the active ingredient is glyphosate are completely satisfactory as they are inactivated on contact with the soil. When using a systemic herbicide, timing of the application is vital. Such herbicides work on the principle of being absorbed by the plant tissue and then translocated around the sap stream, killing the plant completely without polluting the soil. The herbicide need only come into contact with a portion of the foliage in order to be totally effective. This is in contrast to the more traditional contact killers which depend upon blanket coverage of the foliage to be completely effective.

The most effective time to apply a systemic herbicide is in the spring when the weeds are making active growth. At this time there is sufficient leafy cover which is receptive to the herbicide and the sap will take the poison to all parts of the plant most quickly. But although this means of weed killing does not pollute the site, it does demand a degree of patience, for systemic herbicides take several weeks to work effectively. If nothing much appears to happen for the first couple of weeks take heart, for it does not indicate failure. Certainly resist the temptation of seeking rapid action by applying a contact killer. Burning off the foliage will reduce the effectiveness of a previously applied systemic herbicide and may not reach an underground root system.

It should also be remembered that although the herbicide will kill plants completely, their destroyed tissue will remain brown and intact for some time. This is often difficult to cope with, for many of the pernicious weeds of damp places are tough and form large clumps. While it may be tempting to remove all the brown foliage debris early on, it is more prudent to leave it for a few weeks to let it start decomposing. Once the dead foliage has started to rot and the tussocks of clump-forming plants become loose and detach readily, then the entire area can be scarified with a strong rake and the old vegetation removed. Cultivation can then commence with a view to planting shortly afterwards.

CHAPTER 2

THE WATERSIDE

Although few gardeners are fortunate enough to have a natural stream running through their property, such an asset should be exploited, especially if it is a stream with a constant year-round flow of water. A stream is different from any other feature, for it only belongs to you while it is running through your garden. Upstream and downstream belong to someone else, so very little can be done to alter its course or rate of flow without affecting neighbours. Indeed, if the stream is of local importance it is imprudent to interfere with it for fear of causing localized flooding or drought.

STEPPING STONES

Stepping stones placed at strategic intervals are the safest means of altering the effect of flowing water. Strategically placed, these can create a calm area beside either bank so that aquatic plants can become established much more quickly.

Stepping stones should be large enough to accommodate a good-sized foot if they are also to serve as a crossing place. When local stone is available this should be used, but avoid limestone as this erodes quickly, and sandstone, which can be badly shaled by frost. If suitable stone is difficult to come by, then it is possible to make artificial stepping stones easily and cheaply. In an area of open ground dig holes the size and shape of the desired stones. Mix one part by volume of cement to three parts by volume of aggregate and pour this into the holes. When the 'stones' have set, they can be dug up and placed in position. Within a short space of time they will start to take on a weathered appearance.

COPING WITH EROSION

Irrespective of whether you decide to alter the flow of your stream, in the course of a season some parts of the bank will tend to erode, particularly where there is no plant cover. This happens most frequently during the winter months when the water level can rise quickly and the rate of water flow increase alarmingly. It is a particularly common occurrence just before or after a bend. Bends throw the current's main flow from the centre to the edge and lead to erosion by scouring or by undermining the base of the bank so that the top subsides. Sheet erosion of the top soil also occurs near bends but attempts to correct this can be made by

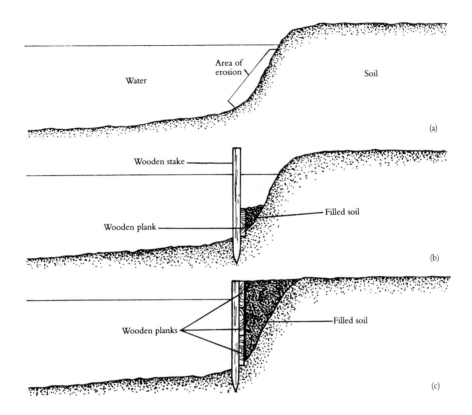

Fig. 4 *Dealing with erosion of bank*
(a) Fast-flowing or turbulent streams quickly cause bank erosion, even when planted.
(b) Stakes firmly hammered into the stream bed at the base of the eroded bank provide support for protective planking.
(c) As each plank is put in place, fill with soil to trap it against its support. Continue until above maximum water level.

artificial means.

Wood and steel are the most frequently used materials. Do not use concrete as this is an uncompromising material that is rigid and incapable of satisfactorily withstanding the often opposing pressures of soil and water. It is also extremely difficult to disguise. Wood is probably the easiest material to work with and is not displeasing to the eye. By driving in stakes and erecting boards in the water close by the muddy edge (Fig. 4), it is often possible to reclaim an area of rich silt which, if mixed with a little ordinary garden soil, provides a first-class medium for growing moisture-loving plants.

PREPARATIONS FOR PLANTING

Handling primary erosion is one thing, cultivating stream banks and coping with the increased potential erosion problems is quite another. As soon as cultivation starts, erosion begins, unless you take unconventional steps to prevent it.

Before they are cultivated, most stream banks have a covering of wild plants, but many of these plants are deep-rooted and invasive, often to the point of choking a small shallow stream, so if you wish to replant with more controllable, attractive species, the ground will first have to be cleared.

It is a complete waste of time planting into soil that contains any pernicious weeds. These become entangled in the desirable plants and are more difficult to remove from wet soil than from the ordinary bed or border. If this happens the plants all have to be lifted and every vestige of perennial root removed, otherwise they serve as reservoirs of future infestation.

Since the roots of the weeds hold the bank together and prevent the soil from being displaced, the initial idea should be to kill the plant growth, but allow the old roots to remain in place to bind the soil on the bank.

Begin in the spring by applying a systemic herbicide with glyphosate as the active ingredient. All the plant tissue will be killed, but will leave no harmful residue as glyphosate is devoured by micro-organisms in the soil. Allow the weed top growth to collapse and decompose back into the soil. Once decomposition has started, apply a generous mulch of well-rotted animal manure or garden compost over the entire surface of the sprayed area. This smothers any seedling weeds and during the course of the summer also decomposes and forms a rich organic medium for planting the following spring. This surface medium comprises the mulch and the decomposed remains of the original weedcover, but at the same time the old roots of that weed growth, although dead, are still binding banks together. Providing that planting takes place during the following spring, then the roots of the new streamside plants will take over the role of binding the soil to prevent future erosion.

GRASSING A BANK

It is not always desirable to plant a stream side completely with decorative plants. A grassy bank sweeping down to a rippling stream can be equally attractive. Achieving such an effect is not always so easy, for as little cultivation as possible will be necessary if the grass is to be established without problems of erosion. This is certainly the case when a grassy area is being started from seed.

Irrespective of whether seed or turf is used the banks must be only lightly cultivated. Landscape contractors are able to purchase a fine weave matting to peg to vulnerable areas which allows grass to grow through, but the home

Variegated foliage provides a long-lasting highlight at the streamside.

This stream provides a colourful backbone for the garden.

gardener has little option except to use fine garden netting. The kind used for windbreaks is quite suitable. Peg the netting firmly to the soil from below minimum water level to above expected high water level. Turf can then be laid over the top, or a little compost scattered over the netting and seeds sown into this. In both cases the grassy bank will be stabilized.

PLANTING BESIDE A STREAM OR POOL

Spring is the perfect time to plant all moisture-loving plants, ideally just as they are showing signs of breaking into growth. The only exceptions are the irises. These much prefer to be moved immediately after flowering, although they are tolerant of spring planting. Arrange plants in groups, unless a giant feature plant like a rheum or gunnera is being placed, when an individual plant is sufficient. Odd numbers are always easiest to arrange, five being ideal for most situations, but with smaller areas three is often enough because of the limitations of space.

Most plants are now pot grown. When they fill the pots with roots, but the rootballs still have a little give in them when gently squeezed, they should be planted without disturbance. When the rootball is solid, it is prudent to take a sharp knife and make three or four cuts from top to bottom to allow the roots to break out. Often, if allowed to remain in a congested mass, the roots do not spread out properly and ramify into the surrounding soil. The rootball just develops a fuzz of bristly, whisker-like hair roots and the growth of the plant is restricted, much as if it were still in a pot. Such plants have usually been left in their pots too long and are ripe for dividing. The thrifty gardener will look at plants like this on the beds in the garden centre and select those that clearly have two or three crowns. These can be readily divided at planting time and will be just as good as younger pot–grown specimens.

Once planted, regular watering is vital until the plants are well established. A generous mulch of well-rotted animal manure or garden compost is invaluable in conserving moisture and suppressing weed growth. None of the plants described in this book warrants canes or stakes for support. Indeed, such paraphernalia rests ill at ease in a waterside feature. All plants, once established, should be sufficiently close together that they provide mutual support.

Consideration so far has been given to waterside planting in a moist and amenable soil. In many cases this is the situation, although the rise and fall of water in a stream or a planted drainage ditch can create considerable variations in soil moisture content. This has to be coped with by the application of water in times of drought and compensated for as far as possible by the liberal incorporation of organic matter into the soil and the addition of a generous surface mulch.

Very often, however, the waterside conditions are not as straightforward as this. If a pool or stream has been contrived with artificial materials like a liner or concrete, then the soil around may get very dry. Yet to create a pleasing effect, plants that appear to be moisture lovers needed to be grown beyond the confines of the water to mask the edge and complete the scene. Visit a garden centre and look for plants that are tolerant of ordinary drier soil conditions but which have the general architectural character of waterside plants. It is a complete waste of time to plant waterside plants anywhere but in very moist conditions in the hope that you can keep them going. Even if you have ready access to a hosepipe, no ban on its use and the time and will to use it regularly, the planting rarely comes off properly.

Where harsh edges have to be masked, it is simpler to position the plants within the pool or stream and allow them to tumble out. Scrambling plants like water mint (*Mentha aquatica*), brooklime (*Veronica beccabunga*) and creeping Jenny (*Lysimachia nummularia*) are fine examples that will do the job properly and create a most pleasing effect. These plants will need a suitable ledge just below the water level on which to place containers or compost, but even where this was not incorporated in the original plan, it should not be impossible to contrive an arrangement where such plants can be established. Ordinary herbaceous plants, such as *Tradescantia virginiana* 'Isis', *Libertia formosa* or *Sysyrinchium striatum*, can also be planted further out and the two types can intermingle to produce a most satisfying effect.

While the choice of plants and their association with one another are very much a matter of personal taste, it should be remembered that all bog and moisture-loving plants die back during the winter. Some disappear completely, leaving the bog garden or waterside a desert of dark soil or mud, nothing lightening the darkness until the marsh marigolds burst into growth into early spring. To counter this, introduce one or two woody plants. The coloured-stemmed cornus and the garden willows that respond to stooling or cutting back will not only add height and structure to the bog garden or waterside during the winter, but provide colour where there would otherwise be none.

CHAPTER 3

MARGINAL PLANTS

Marginal plants are those that will tolerate standing in water for all or much of the year. They are popularly planted on the narrow ledges that surround garden pools, but of course are invaluable for streamside planting, especially where there is constant water, even if the level is variable. Some varieties are invasive when in a situation to their liking, so consideration should be given either to omitting them completely or restricting root activity. The result of the latter is often poorer quality plants. However, an invasive tendency can be used to advantage when erosion is a problem, rapidly growing matted rootstocks being the finest method of preventing soil being washed away. Among the diversity of marginal plants available there is something for everyone and for every situation. All the plants described here will tolerate anything from moist soil to 10 cm (4 in) of water, some of the taller kinds being able to cope with a depth of up to 20 cm (8 in).

Acorus calamus (Sweet flag)
Long, fresh green, sword-like leaves arise from a fat, fleshy rootstock. They smell of tangerines when bruised and support strange yellowish green horn-like flower spikes. Easily increased by division during the growing season. 90 cm (3 ft).
A.c. 'Variegatus'   This variety retains the bold sword-shaped leaves of the species, but they are handsomely variegated with cream, green and rose, the latter colour being particularly evident during the spring. Rarely flowers. Propagation by division during the growing season. 60–90 cm (6 in).

Acorus gramineus
A dwarf, grassy-leafed species with very dark green foliage. Flowers insignificant. Easily increased by division during the growing season. 15 cm (6 in).
A.g. 'Variegatus'   A variety with cream and dark green foliage. Susceptible to frost damage during severe winters. Increase by division during the growing season. 15 cm (6 in)

Alisma parviflora
A water plantain with rounded leaf blades on strong leaf stalks. Shorter, neater heads of white, or sometimes pink, blossoms. The dried heads of this species are not as spectacular as those of *A. plantago-aquatica*, but are worth preserving. Propagation by seed sown immediately it ripens. 30–75 cm (1–2½ ft).

Alisma plantago-aquatica (Water plantain)

A bold marginal aquatic with attractive ovate, bright green foliage and loose pyramidal panicles of pink and white flowers. These flower heads become hard and woody after flowering and are first class for winter decoration indoors. They produce very viable seed, which if allowed to disperse unchecked, will rapidly yield choking masses of seedlings. Propagation by seed sown as soon as it has ripened. 60–90 cm (2–3 ft)

Alisma ranunculoides

A creeping plant of dwarf stature, with delicate arching stems which bend down and root wherever they touch moist soil. Rapidly forms a spreading colony of bright green lance-shaped foliage, sprinkled with crowded umbels of rose or blush flowers during late summer and early autumn. 15 cm (6 in).

Butomus umbellatus (Flowering bush)

A lovely rush-like marginal plant with handsome bright green foliage. Beautiful showy pink blossoms produced in spreading umbels during late summer. Grows from a creeping rootstock that is host to masses of small bulbils, each capable of producing a new plant if removed and transplanted independently. Propagation by the removal of bulbils in the spring or by division of established plants during the spring or early summer. 60–90 cm (2–3 ft).

Calla palustris (Bog arum)

An excellent plant for disguising the unsightly edge of a pool or artificially contrived bog garden. It has a strong creeping rootstock and is clothed in handsome, glossy, heart-shaped foliage. The white blossoms are rather like small sails. These are followed by dense spikes of succulent orange-red fruits which persist into autumn. Propagation is by cutting the creeping rootstock into short sections in early spring. Each section should have a bud. These are then planted in trays of mud or very wet compost. Seed can be sown immediately after ripening and will usually produce young plants the following spring. 15–30 cm (6–12 in).

Caltha leptosepala (Mountain marigold)

Broad, white, saucer-shaped blossoms with a distinctive silvery tinge are produced above handsome dark green foliage during late spring. Easily increased by division, or seed when this is sown immediately after ripening. 15–45 cm (6–18 in).

Caltha palustris (Marsh marigold)

One of the loveliest marginal aquatics for early spring, growing in damp soil or as much as 30 cm (12 in) of water. Dark green mounds of glossy, scalloped, dark green foliage smothered in bright golden yellow, waxy, saucer-shaped blossoms.

Propagation by seed sown immediately after ripening or division during the growing season. 30–60 cm (1–2 ft).

C. p. alba (White marsh marigold).   Flowers white with golden centres and borne above glossy green leaves during late spring. Unfortunately this suffers badly from mildew and is best replaced wherever possible by *C. leptosepela*. Propagation by division of the plants during the growing season. 30–45 cm (12–18 in).

C. p. 'Flore Pleno' (Double marsh marigold) Fully double, bright golden yellow blossoms like small pompom chrysanthemums during spring and early summer. Neat, tight mounds of bright green glossy foliage. Can only be increased by division during the growing period. 15–30 cm (6–12 in).

Caltha polypetala (Himalayan marsh marigold)

A very large species requiring plenty of space. Big, bold hummocks of foliage, the individual dark green leaves being as much as 25 cm (10 in) across. Large trusses of bright golden yellow blossoms during late spring. Propagation by division during the growing season or by seed sown immediately after ripening. 60–90 cm (2–3 ft).

Cotula coronopifolia (Brass buttons)

Produces masses of bright yellow rounded heads of flowers all summer long, above a solid mass of strongly scented light green foliage. Unfortunately *C. coronopifolia* is monocarpic and therefore dies after flowering. However, there is usually sufficient seed scattered around to ensure continuity. It is wise to clip the seed heads off before the seeds ripen and thereby exercise some control over their distribution, at the same time preserving a small group of plants so that seed can be gathered for sowing under controlled conditions the following spring. 15 cm (6 in).

Damasonium alisma (Starfruit)

Green strap-shaped leaves arise from a hard corm-like rootstock. Spikes of milky white flowers during summer are followed by curious star-shaped fruits. Large clumps can be divided during the growing season, but it is more usual to increase this plant from seed sown immediately it ripens. 15–20 cm (6–8 in).

Houttuynia cordata

An easily grown creeping plant for the shallow margins of the pool or the bog garden. This is so adaptable that it can be grown even in a damp spot in the herbaceous border. Bluish-green heart-shaped leaves with a maroon or purplish caste produce a somewhat acrid smell when crushed. The flowers are creamy white, four-petalled and have a hard white central cone. Ideal for carpeting the bare earth among taller growing plants. Propagation is by division of established plants during early spring. 15–30 cm (6–12 in).

H. c. 'Plena' Similar to the common single-flowered species, but with

flowers which have dense central ruff of petals. A much more decorative plant. Propagation by division of established plants during spring. 15–30 cm (6–12 in).
H. c. 'Variegata' A very popular form with darker purplish green leaves splashed with yellow and cream. Flowers sparsely. Propagation by division of established plants during spring. 15–30 cm (6–12 in).

Hypericum elodes (Marsh hypericum)
Although a relative of the popular garden rose of Sharon, this little plant tolerates bog garden conditions or even shallow water. A first class carpeting plant for disguising difficult areas at the pool or waterside. Small green leaves studded with small bright yellow, saucer-shaped flowers. Propagation by seed sown during the spring, division during early spring or stem cuttings during the summer months. 8–15 cm (3–6 in).

Iris laevigata
This is the true blue-flowered aquatic iris. An easy plant to establish, forming clumps of sword-shaped smooth green leaves and blossoming during early summer. There are a number of cultivars, all of which should be increased by division immediately after flowering. Seed can be sown during spring or early summer, but the flower colour of the resulting plants is likely to be variable. 60–90 cm (2–3 ft).
I. l. 'Alba' A pure white-flowered cultivar. 60–90 cm (2–3 ft).
I. l. 'Atropurpurea' A vivid purple-blue cultivar. Free-flowering. 60–75 cm (2–2½ ft).
I. l. 'Colchesteri' Large flowered with violet-purple and white blossoms. Often available under the name 'Monstrosum'. 60–90 cm (2–3 ft).
I. l. 'Mottled Beauty' White blossom liberally mottled with blue. 60–90 cm (2–3 ft).
I. l. 'Muragumo' A beautiful free-flowering cultivar with six prominent petals rather than three. Blue petals sport gold reticulations. 60 cm (2 ft).
I. l. 'Regal' Lovely magenta-flowered iris. 60–75 cm (2–2½ ft).
I. l. 'Rose Queen' Soft pink flowers and pale green leaves. 60–75 cm (2–2½ ft).
I. l. 'Semperflorens' A free-flowering blue variety. 60–90 cm (2–3 ft).
I. l. 'Snowdrift' Large-flowered cultivar with pure white blossoms. Bold green sword-like leaves. 60–90 cm (2–3 ft).
I. l. 'Variegata' Small blue flowers, but the most startling gold and green variegated foliage. Rarely attains a height of more than 75 cm (2½ ft).
I. l. 'Violet Parasol' Large-flowered violet blue variety. 60–90 cm (2–3 ft).

Iris pseudacorus (Yellow flag)
A very vigorous and easily grown iris that is only suitable for gardens where there is plenty of space. Most useful for wildlife gardens. It has yielded a number of

interesting and useful cultivars. Tall mid-green strap-like leaves and bright yellow blossoms with small black markings during the summer. Easily increased by seed sown during the spring or early summer, or division immediately after flowering. 75–90 cm (2½–3 ft). All the cultivars recommended below must be increased by division.

I. p. var. bastardii Not such a vigorous plant as the species, but equally bulky. Creamy yellow flowers among bold sword-shaped foliage. 75–90 cm (2½–3 ft).

***I. p.* 'Beuron'** A recently introduced yellow-flowered tetraploid cultivar. 75–90 cm (2½–3 ft).

***I. p.* 'Flora–Plena'** A double-flowered form of the common yellow flag. A slightly more restrained and generally more colourful plant than the species. 75–90 cm (2½–3 ft).

***I. p.* 'Golden Queen'** Of more modest proportions than the common

A well-manicured lawn provides a pleasant foil for irises and other moisture-loving plants.

species. A selection with more refined golden blossoms in greater numbers. Bold sword-shaped green leaves. 75–90 cm (2½–3 ft).

I. p. 'Sulphur Queen' Beautiful sulphurous yellow flowers freely produced among bold sword-shaped green foliage. 75–90 cm (2½–3 ft).

I. p. 'Variegata' Handsome cream and green, sword-shaped leaves which are startlingly effective during late spring and early summer. These gradually fade to pale green, during which time the yellow flowers are produced. A much slower growing plant than the species, and of more modest habit. 60–75 cm (2–2½ ft).

Iris versicolor

The blossoms of this fine iris are produced during early summer and are violet blue veined with purple with a conspicuous patch of yellow on the falls. Leaves mid-green and sword-shaped. Easily increased from seed sown during spring or early summer, or division after flowering. Seed raised plants will produce flowers of variable colour and quality. 60–75 cm (2–2½ ft). Like *I. pseudacorus*, its cultivars should all be increased by division.

I. v. 'Alba' A white-flowered selection. 60–75 cm (2–2½ ft).

I. v. 'Claret Cup' An attractive deep claret purple flowered cultivar. 60–75 cm (2–2½ ft).

I. v. 'Kermesina' The most popular and widely grown cultivar. Beautifully marked and veined blossoms of deep plum with petals of satin-like quality. Bold green sword-like leaves. 60–75 cm (2–2½ ft).

I. v. 'Rosea' A rose-purple selection. 60–75 cm (2–2½ ft).

Lysichiton americanum (Skunk cabbage)

A member of the arum family with bright yellow spathes which appear during early spring, well ahead of the large green cabbagey foliage. Increase from seed sown immediately it ripens in a tray of mud or wet compost. It is very difficult to divide skunk cabbages even though they are clump-forming plants. When this is attempted it should be done in the spring before they come into flower. 60–90 cm (2–3 ft).

Lysichiton camtschatcense (White flowered Japanese skunk cabbage)

Rather smaller than its American cousin and much less impressive. Increase from seed sown immediately it ripens. 60–90 cm (2–3 ft).

Mentha aquatica (Water mint)

An easy-going and occasionally rampant plant for shallow water or the bog garden. When used sensibly, the water mint can tie the pool and the surrounding ground together, completely disguising the harsh pool edge. It will grow in shallow water or just damp soil, scrambling about and rooting at almost every leaf joint. It is heavily aromatic, with dense, rounded, hairy, green foliage on slender reddish stems; soft lilac-pink blossoms like miniature powder puffs appear in mid and late summer. Increase easily by early spring division or by taking soft stem cuttings during the summer months. 30–45 cm (12–18 in).

Menyanthes trifoliata (Bog bean)

This produces showy white-fringed flowers during spring above dark green foliage somewhat reminiscent of a broad bean. Both the leaves and flowers rise from a sprawling olive green stem. If this is chopped into sections, each with a root attached, new plants are easily produced. 20–30 cm (8–12 in).

Mimulus luteus (Yellow musk)

Soft green rounded foliage and bright yellow spikes of blossoms not unlike those of an antirrhinum. It flowers for much of the summer and is ver y easily increased from seed sown during spring or early summer, or by division of the over-wintered rosettes in spring. 20–30 cm (8–12 in).

Mimulus ringens

A delicate-looking plant with many-branched slender stems and handsome narrow green leaflets. Flowers are somewhat tubular, lavender to blue and produced freely along the spiky stems in summer. Easily raised from seed sown in pans of mud under glass during early spring. Soft stem cuttings taken during the summer also root readily. 45 cm (18 in).

Myosotis scorpioides (Water forget-me-not)

This is a perennial aquatic version of the popular bedding forget-me-not. Unlike that species, the water forget-me-not has smooth leaves and less compact heads of light blue flowers which are produced for much of the summer. Easily increased from seed sown during the spring, the plants should ideally be raised in small pots in a frame where they can be stood in a tray of water. 20 cm (8 in).

M. s. var. alba   A white form that often occurs in seed-raised plants. Seed saved from this rarely comes true, so white-flowered plants should be increased by division. 20 cm (8 in).

M. s. 'Semperflorens'   A more compact and free-flowering seed-raised selection of the species. 20 cm (8 in).

Peltandra alba (Arrow arum)

An interesting member of the arum family. Dark green, arrow-like, glossy green foliage, with narrow whitish green spathes in summer sometimes followed by reddish fruits. Easily increased by division during early spring. 45 cm (18 in).

Peltandra virginica

A very similar plant but with less showy and narrower greenish spathes during summer. Easily increased by division in early spring. 45–60 cm (1½–2 ft).

Pontederia cordata (Pickerel)

A handsome plant producing numerous stems each consisting of an oval or lance-shaped shiny green leaf and a leafy bract from which the spike of soft blue flowers appears during late summer. Propagation is by seed sown immediately it ripens. Spring division of the crowns of established plants is also effective. Do not divide the plants until they are seen to be actively growing. 60–90 cm (2–3 ft).

Pontederia lanceolata
Very similar to the common pickerel, but larger in every part and with bold lance-shaped foliage. Flowers are blue and in neat spikes. 90–120 cm (3–4 ft).

Preslia cervina
A lovely plant forming spreading clumps of slender erect stems densely clothed in small lance-shaped leaves and crowned during late summer with stiff whorled spikes of dainty ultramarine or lilac flowers. The whole plant is aromatic and happiest when growing in shallow water or very wet soil. Easily increased by short stem cuttings taken during spring and inserted in pots of very wet compost. 30 cm (12 in).

Ranunculus flammula (Lesser spearwort)
Early summer-flowering buttercup-like plant with glistening golden flowers above dark green, roughly oval leaves and slender reddish scrambling stems. An ideal plant for masking the dividing line between pool and bog. Propagation is by separating the emerging shoots during early spring and planting them out individually. 25–30 cm (10–12 in).

Ranunculus lingua (Greater spearwort)
A lovely tall-growing buttercup with strong, red-flushed, erect hollow stems well clothed with dark green leaves. Easily increased by early spring division of the rootstock. 60–90 cm (2–3 ft).
R. l. 'Grandiflora' This is the plant that is sold by most aquatic specialists. A much improved form in every respect. Increased by early spring division of the creeping rootstock. 60–90 cm (2–3 ft).

Rumex hydrolapathum (Water dock)
A tall-growing plant for the wildlife garden. An enlarged version of the common garden dock, but with bold dark green foliage that changes from green to bronze and crimson at the approach of autumn. Easily increased from seed sown during the spring or else division just as the plant starts to break into growth. Up to 3 m (10 ft).
R. h. var. *maximus* This form is slightly smaller, but with much larger individual leaves which have the same autumnal hues. Over 2 m (7 ft).

Sagittaria japonica (Japanese arrowhead)
Broad, light green, arrow-shaped foliage and bold spikes of papery white single flowers with conspicuous yellow centres. These are produced from mid to late summer. Propagation is by dividing clumps of growing plants during the

A rock stream is ideal for mimulus and primulas.

summer or separating out dormant winter buds. 45–60 cm (1½–2 ft).
S. j. 'Flore Pleno' (Double Japanese arrowhead)   Fully double blossoms, rather like small white powder puffs. 45–60 cm (1½–2 ft).

Sagittaria latifolia
Bold arrow-shaped leaves from among which pure white blossoms are produced. Prefers slightly acid conditions. Easily increased by summer division or redistribution of winter buds during the dormant period. 90–120 cm (3–4 ft).
S. l. 'Flore Pleno'   Fully double white flowers. Propagation by the redistribution of winter buds. 90–10 cm (3–4 ft).

Sagittaria sagittifolia (Arrowhead)
White papery-petalled blossoms with black centres appear during late summer. Propagation by division of growing plants or the redistribution of dormant winter buds. 45–60 cm (1½–2 ft).

Saururus cernuus (Lizard's tail)
A bizarre aquatic plant for shallow water or bog. It produces strong-growing clumps of heart-shaped foliage which often take on bright flame tints in autumn. The flowers are creamy white and produced in quaint nodding terminal sprays during the summer. Easily increased by division during early spring. 30 cm (12 in).

Veronica beccabunga (Brooklime)
Dark blue flowers with a white eye are produced in profusion in the axils of the leaves. The foliage is dark green, rounded and liberally clothes rapidly growing scrambling stems. Flowers throughout the summer and although not strictly speaking evergreen, retains its foliage for much of the year. Easily increased by short stem cuttings rooted in pans of mud or wet compost. 15–20 cm (6–8 in).

CHAPTER 4

BOG OR MARSH PLANTS

It is difficult to say exactly where the dividing line is between bog or marsh plants and those that we regard as marginals. Nature has given us no firm guidelines, but gardeners generally deem those plants which can be grown in containers on the marginal shelf of a pool as marginal plants, whereas bog or marsh plants embrace all the others that enjoy wet or damp conditions, from the real bog plants of muddy banks to those perennials that must have constant year-round moisture to give of their best and are sometimes seen in the herbaceous border. Many are naturally plants of stream or riversides and used to variations in soil moisture content, from temporary winter inundation to relative summer dryness. Neither situation is desirable for any length of time, but all those plants described here will tolerate both extremes for a brief spell and are easily accommodated in most gardens.

Aconitum napellus (Monkshood)
Erect spikes of hooded navy blue flowers above mounds of glossy green, deeply cut foliage during summer. Can be easily increased from a summer sowing of seed, although it divides quite readily during the winter or early spring. 1.2–1.5 cm (4–5 ft). The varieties listed below should all be propagated by division.

A. n. **'Bicolor'**   A bi-coloured form with blue and white hooded flowers. Foliage glossy green, deeply cut. 90–120 cm (3–4 ft).

A. n. **'Bressingham Spire'**   A stocky plant with violet blue blossoms in dense spikes. 90 cm (3 ft).

A. n. **'Carneum'**   Shell pink flowers and glossy green, deeply cut foliage. 90 cm (3 ft).

A. n. **'Grandiflorum Album'**   White flowers, deeply cut glossy green foliage. 90 cm (3 ft).

A. n. **'Spark's Variety'**   An excellent violet blue monkshood with beautiful large blossoms in bold spikes. Handsome green foliage. 90 cm (3 ft).

Aconitum wilsonii
Tall spires of bright blue hooded flowers above dark green three-lobed leaves. A most useful bog plant as it extends the flowering season into autumn. Increased by division during the winter or early spring. 1.2–1.8 m (4–6 ft).

Aconitum vulparia (Wolfsbane)

An untidy scrambling mound of finely cut dark green foliage, bright throughout the summer with short spikes of soft yellow blossoms. Increased by seed or division during the winter or early summer. 90–120 cm (3–4 ft).

Ajuga pyramidalis

A scrambling plant that is excellent for the pool or streamside. Flourishes in wet soil, but is also capable of existing in moderately damp garden soil. Plain green leaves. During summer it is smothered with short spikes of bright gentian-blue flowers. Easily increased by division of plantlets during spring. 15–30 cm (6–12 in).

A. p. 'Metallica' A very fine foliage plant with leaves of a deep metallic bronze. Flowers are an intense blue. Easily increased by division of plantlets during spring. 15–30 cm (6–12 in).

Ajuga reptans **'Burgundy Glow'**

A glowing rosy-leaved variety of the common bugle. 15 cm (6 in)

A. r. 'Jungle Beauty' The tallest and most vigorous of this group of bugles. Plain green leaves and spikes of intense blue flowers. Readily increased by separating plantlets during early spring. 15–30 cm (6–12 in).

A. r. 'Purpurea' Deep purple-bronze foliage and short spikes of blue flowers. Increased by separating plantlets during early spring. 15 cm (6 in).

A. r. 'Rainbow' A multi-coloured foliage form with pink, green and cream leaves. Blue flowers in short spikes during summer. Increased by separating plantlets during early spring. 15 cm (6 in).

Anemone rivularis

Loose umbels of snow-white flowers with bright violet anthers in spring or early summer. Handsome, somewhat downy, toothed foliage which arises from a swollen rootstock. Increased from seed. 30–60 cm (1–2 ft).

Anemone virginiana

The best anemone for really wet conditions. Soon forms clumps of toothed green leaves from among which emerge clusters of greenish white or greenish purple flowers during early summer. Best propagated from seed. 45–90 cm (1½–3 ft).

Anemopsis californica (Apache beads)

A plant of anemone-like appearance with flowers that consist of a hard cone surrounded by a single whorl of pearly white petal-like bracts. Enjoys really wet alkaline conditions. Propagate by division of established clumps during spring, or by seed when this is available. 30–45 cm (12–18 in).

Anthericum liliago (St Bernard's lily)

A beautiful summer-flowering perennial with tufts of narrow grassy foliage from among which are produced slender spikes of elegant, tubular white flowers. Increase by division during early spring or else seed sown immediately it ripens. 60 cm (2 ft).

Aruncus dioicus (Goat's beard)

A tall, handsome plant rather like an astilbe, with bold plumes of creamy white flowers during late summer. The leaves are pale green, deeply cut and lobed and produced on stems rather reminiscent of bamboo canes. Easily increased by division during the dormant period. Providing that each piece of root has a shoot or bud it should grow. 90–150 cm (3–5 ft).

A. d. 'Kneiffii' A more compact plant well suited to the smaller garden. Creamy white plumes of blossom arise from deeply divided green foliage. Increased by division during the dormant period. 90 cm (3 ft).

Asclepias incarnata (Swamp milkweed)

A much neglected waterside plant that prospers in really damp situations. Stout leafy stems are crowned with crowded umbels of rose-pink flowers during summer. Can be increased by division during early spring. 60–90 cm (2–3 ft).

A. i. var. alba This has white blossoms but is otherwise similar to A. *incarnata*. Lance-shaped green leaves and typical crowded flowerheads. 60–90 cm (2–3 ft).

Aster puniceus (Swamp aster)

A rather unruly plant with reddish stems and rough, hairy foliage. Very showy flowers during late summer or early autumn of lilac or pale violet purple rather like those of a Michaelmas daisy. Can be increased from seed, but more readily by division of the rootstocks in early spring just as they start to shoot. 90–150 cm (3–5 ft).

Astilbe × *arendsii* 'Fanal'

One of the most striking and popular astilbes. Plumes of deep crimson flowers during mid and late summer above neat mounds of deeply cut, dark green foliage. Increased by division of the rootstocks during the dormant period. 30–45 cm (12–18 in).

A. × a. 'Irrlicht' A lovely, icy-cool white-flowered cultivar with dark green foliage. Increased by division of the rootstock during the dormant period. 60–75 cm (2–2½ ft).

A. × a. 'Ostrich Plume' Rich pink flowers in lean feathery spikes. Green divided foliage. Increased by division of the rootstock during the dormant period. 75–90 cm (2½–3 ft).

A natural rill well clothed with permanent planting.

***A. × a.* 'Peach Blossom'**   Salmon pink flowers in feathery plumes above deeply divided green leaves. Increased by division of the rootstock during the dormant period. 60–90 cm (2–3 ft).

***A. × a.* 'White Gloria'**   A pure white-flowered variety of compact habit. Green divided foliage. Increased by division of the rootstock during the dormant winter period. 60–75 cm (2–2½ ft).

Astilbe chinensis 'Pumila'

A charming short-growing cultivar with low, spreading mats of dark green somewhat ferny foliage, which during late summer become a mass of bright pinkish mauve flower spikes. Increased by division of the rootstock during the dormant period. 30–45 cm (12–18 in).

Astilbe crispa 'Lilliput'

A charming small plant that enables the gardener with the tiniest bog garden or poolside to enjoy astilbes. Congested tufts of dark green crinkled foliage and tightly packed spires of salmon pink flowers during late summer. Increased by division of the rootstock during the winter months. 15 cm (6 in).

***A. c.* 'Perkeo'**   Very similar to *A. c.* 'Lilliput', but with tightly packed spikes of intense deep pink flowers. Dark green congested foliage. Increased by division of the rootstock during the winter months. 15 cm (6 in).

Buphthalmum salicifolium

An attractive, but somewhat unruly character with hairy, green lance-shaped leaves and heads of yellow daisy flowers produced during summer. Propagated from seed sown during the spring, or division of the rootstock during the dormant period. 45–60 cm (1½–2 ft).

Buphthalmum speciosum

An unusual plant with large, drooping, daisy-like yellow flowers during summer. Hairy, green, somewhat aromatic foliage. Easily raised from spring-sown seed or division of the rootstock during the dormant period. 90–120 cm (3–4 ft).

Cardamine pratensis (Cuckoo flower)

A charming spring-flowering perennial for the waterside. Single rosy-lilac flowers are produced in abundance above tufts of pale green ferny foliage. Easily increased by seed or, when necessary, by division during the dormant period. 30–45 cm (12–18 in).

C. p. flore plena   A fully double form of more compact growth. This must be increased by division during the dormant period. 30 cm (12 in).

Cornus alba (Red-barked dogwood)

A thicket-forming shrub with red stems and green leaves that change to copper and gold in the autumn. If pruned to the ground each spring it is unlikely to flower. Grown predominantly for its coloured stems. Increase by hardwood cuttings taken during the winter. 120 m (4 ft) if pruned back each spring.

C. a. 'Sibirica'   A less vigorous cultivar with brilliant red stems during the winter if regularly stooled each spring. Propagate from hardwood cuttings during the winter. 90–120 cm (3–4 ft) if stooled annually.

C. a. 'Spaethii'   This cultivar has winter stems almost as showy as *C. a.* 'Sibirica' and the added bonus of handsome gold and green variegated foliage in the summer. Propagate from hardwood cuttings taken during the winter. 90–120 cm (3–4 ft) if stooled annually.

Cornus stolonifera 'Flaviramea'
A handsome shrub that also needs regularly stooling to give of its best. Bright yellow to olive green stems during winter. 90–120 cm (3–4 ft) if stooled annually.

Eupatorium ageratoides
A bold, branching perennial with coarsely toothed leaves and numerous pure white blossoms in compound heads. Flowers during summer and is easily increased by division of the rootstock during early spring. 60–120 cm (2–4 ft).

Eupatorium cannabinum (Hemp agrimony)
A plant for the wildlife area rather than the tidy formal garden. Downy, toothed foliage is smothered during the summer with terminal clusters of reddish purple flowers. Propagated by division of the rootstock in early spring. 60–120 cm (2–4 ft).

Eupatorium purpureum (Joe Pyeweed)
A coarse-leaved perennial with crowded heads of small purple flowers during late summer and early autumn. Increased by division of the rootstock during early spring. 120 cm (4 ft).

Euphorbia palustris
Lush green mounds of foliage smothered in yellow-green flowerheads. Best increased from division in the spring, just as young shoots are emerging. 45–90 cm (1½–3 ft).

Filipendula hexapetala (Dropwort)
A relative of the popular meadowsweet (*F. ulmaria*), with most attractive fern-like foliage and stems of tiny creamy white flowers during summer. Increased readily by division of the rootstock in early spring. 60–90 cm (2–3 ft).

F. h. flore-pleno   A fully double form. Increased by division of the rootstock during early spring. 60 cm (2 ft).

Filipendula palmata
Large, lobed, dark green leaves from among which tall slender plumes of tiny pale pink blossoms are produced. These fade to white or off-pink with age. Increased by division of the rootstock during the dormant period. 90 cm (3 ft).

Filipendula purpurea
Large feathery spikes of carmine or deep pink blossoms on crimson flower stems during mid and late summer. Leaves lobed, dark to mid green in tidy mounds. Increased by division of the rootstock during the dormant period. 60–120 cm (2–4 ft).

Filipendula rubra (Queen of the prairie)
An enormous plant with big, bold feathery plumes of deep peach pink blossoms during mid to late summer. Large green leaves significantly lobed and toothed. The variety usually seen in garden centres is 'Magnifica'. Increased by division of the rootstock during the dormant period. 1–2 m (3½–6½ ft).

Filipendula ulmaria (Meadowsweet)
Frothy spires of sweetly scented, creamy white blossoms during mid summer above handsome, deeply cut mid-green foliage. Easily increased from a spring sowing of seed or division of the rootstock during the dormant period. 90–120 cm (3–4 ft).
F. u. 'Aurea' A most startling golden-leaved plant for the bog garden or waterside. Increased by division of the rootstock during the dormant period. 60–90 cm (2–3 ft).
F. u. 'Flore-Pleno' The double-flowered form of the common meadowsweet. Dense feathery spires of sweetly scented, creamy white blossoms during mid summer. Increased by division of the rootstock during the dormant period. 90 cm (3 ft).

Gratiola officinalis (Hedge hyssop)
A useful plant for wilder garden features. It is related to the musks and has fresh green lance-shaped leaves and small white flowers striped with purple. Will grow successfully in standing water as well as moist soil. Easily propagated by division in the spring. 30 cm (12 in).

Gunnera magellanica
A delightful little creeping plant with scalloped kidney-shaped green leaves and odd reddish green flower spikes. This is rarely grown for its horticultural value, but rather as a contrast for the magnificent G. manicata, thus making an interesting conversation piece. Increased by division during early spring. 8 cm (3 in).

Gunnera manicata

Often referred to as giant Brazilian prickly rhubarb. Individual leaves are capable of attaining a diameter of 1.5 m (5 ft) on stems as much as 1.8 m (6 ft) tall. A huge plant in every respect and unfortunately not well suited to the smaller garden. During mid summer an enormous branched flower spike, rather like a huge red-green bottle brush up to 90 cm (3 ft) tall, is produced from a thick procumbent rhizome that is densely clothed in brown papery scales. A South American plant, gunnera often starts into growth quite early. Gardeners in cold frosty locations will usually need to provide some kind of winter protection. This consists of the frosted leaves being placed over the crowns during autumn and secured with pegs and string. The leaves turn crisp and papery, but provide excellent protection from the weather. Propagation is from seed sown immediately it ripens. The crowns can be divided during early spring, each 'nose' with a vestige of root attached being likely to grow on successfully. 1.8–2.4 m (6–8 ft).

Hemerocallis fulva (Day lily)

A vigorous plant that flourishes well in the bog garden or at the waterside. Glossy, pale green grassy foliage and strong flower stems with blossoms of orange or brown. These last a single day, but as there are many buds following a display can be expected for much of the summer. Increased by division of the rootstock during the dormant period. 90 cm–120 cm (3–4 ft). There are now literally thousands of cultivars. Those described here are some of the most popular. All are increased by division of the rootstock during the dormant period.

H. 'Black Prince' Deep velvety-mauve. Slender green foliage. 60–90 cm (2–3 ft).
H. 'Bonanza' Flowers of light orange and maroon-brown. 60–90 cm (2–3 ft).
H. 'Burning Daylight' Rich deep orange blossoms. 60–90 cm (2–3 ft).
H. 'Buzz Bomb' Rich velvety red flowers. 60–90 cm (2–3 ft).
H. 'Chartreuse Magic' Flowers with an unusual combination of canary yellow with an infusion of green. 60–90 cm (2–3 ft).
H. 'Esther Walker' Beautiful rich golden yellow flowers. 60–90 cm (2–3 ft).
H. 'Golden Orchid' Flowers of a deep rich gold. 60–90 cm (2–3 ft).
H. 'Hornby Castle' A very fine cultivar with blossoms of deep brick red and yellow. 60–90 cm (2–3 ft).
H. 'Hyperion' An old favourite with beautiful large lemon yellow blossoms. 90–150 cm (3–5 ft).
H. 'Margaret Perry' A widely cultivated variety with Jaffa orange flowers borne in profusion. 60–90 cm (2–3 ft).
H. 'Marion Vaughan' Bright canary yellow. 60–90 cm (2–3 ft).

H. **'Mikado'**   An old but reliable cultivar with orange blossoms, each with a brown throat. 60–90 cm (2–3 ft).

H. **'Pink Charm'**   A well-tried, small, pink-flowered day lily with slender strap-like leaves. 60–75 cm (2–2½ ft).

H. **'Pink Damask'**   Said to be the best pink currently available. Rose pink and very free-flowering. 60–90 cm (2–3 ft).

H. **'Salmon Sheen'**   Very free-flowering salmon pink. 60–90 cm (2–3 ft).

H. **'Spectacular'**   Golden blossoms with striking bright red centres. 60–90 cm (2–3 ft).

H. **'Stafford'**   An outstanding iridescent red. 60–90 cm (2–3 ft).

H. **'Tejas'**   Smaller flowers than most, but produced in profusion. Deep reddish orange. 60–90 cm (2–3 ft).

H. **'Whichford'**   An outstanding introduction having lemon yellow blossoms with a greenish throat. 60–90 cm (2–3 ft).

Hosta crispula

A foliage plant with oval or lance-shaped green leaves banded with white. Lavender coloured tubular blossoms on slender stems during late summer. Increase by division of the rootstock as soon as growth is observed during early spring. 60–75 cm (2–2½ ft).

Hosta fortunei

Oval leaves of greyish green or green, with tubular lilac to violet flowers during summer. Can be raised from seed, but more usually propagated by division of the rootstock during early spring. 75–90 cm (2½–3 ft).

H. f. **'Albo-picta'**   Similar in most respects to the species, but with a distinctive golden centre to each leaf in spring; the leaves turn completely green by late summer. Propagate by division of the rootstock during early spring. 75–90 cm (2½–3 ft).

H. f. **'Aurea'**   Bright yellow leaves during spring and early summer, which eventually turn green. Increase by division of the rootstock during early spring. 60–75 cm (2–2½ ft).

H. f. **'Aureo-marginata'**   Dark green foliage with persistent gold margins. Increase by division of the rootstock during early spring. 75–90 cm (2½–3 ft).

Hosta lancifolia

Broadly lance-shaped leaves, glossy green and arching. Tubular flowers of deep purple borne on stout flower stems during late summer. Increase by seed sown immediately it ripens or division of the rootstock during early spring. 60 cm (2 ft).

H. l. **'Kabitan'**   A very fine dwarf hosta with bright golden leaves with a green rippled edge. Increase by division during early spring. 30–60 cm (1–2 ft).

Hosta plantaginea
Rounded green leaves and bold spikes of fragrant, pure white trumpet-shaped flowers in late summer. Increase from seed sown immediately after ripening or division of the rootstock during early spring. 60–75 cm (2–2½ ft).

H. p. 'Grandiflora'   A plant with larger leaves and bigger flowers than the ordinary species. Increase by division of the rootstock during early spring. 60–75 cm (2–2½ ft).

H. p. 'Royal Standard'   This is the finest of this group. Large white fragrant blossoms and handsome glossy green leaves. Increase by division of the rootstock during early spring. 60–75 cm (2–2½ ft).

Hosta sieboldiana
Beautiful oval glaucous leaves. Pale lilac tubular flowers on strong flower stalks throughout summer. Seed sown shortly after ripening is a successful method of propagation, but most gardeners prefer to divide the rootstock during early spring. 60–75 cm (2–2½ ft).

H. s. 'Elegans'   Leaves large, much bluer than the species and with a more corrugated surface. Flowers off-white to pale lilac in summer. Increase by division of the rootstock during early spring. 60–75 cm (2–2½ ft).

H. s. 'Mira'   Very much like *H. s.* 'Elegans', but larger in every respect. Increase by division of the rootstock during early spring. 75–90 cm (2½–3 ft).

Hosta tardiflora
A species of similar appearance to *H. lancifolia*, but flowering later. Lance-shaped glossy green leaves and sprays of purple blossoms in the autumn. Increase from seed or division of the rootstock during early spring. 60 cm (2 ft).

Hosta undulata
Small lance-shaped wavy green leaves marked with white. Lilac-coloured tubular blossoms on slender stems during late summer. Propagate by division of rootstock in early spring. 60 cm (2 ft).

H. u. 'Albo-marginata'   Green foliage with distinctive white margins. Increase by division of rootstock during early spring. 60 cm (2 ft).

H. u. 'Erromena'   Strong plain green leaves and lovely lavender-coloured blossoms. Increase by division of the rootstock during early spring. 60 cm (2 ft).

H. u. 'Univittata'   Plain green leaves, each with a prominent white splash in the centre. Must be increased by division of the rootstock in early spring. 60 cm (2 ft).

Hosta ventricosa
Large oval or more or less heart-shaped leaves of deep glossy green. Flowers deep violet and carried on strong stems during summer. Increase from seed sown immediately it ripens or lift and divide the rootstock during early spring. 90 cm (3 ft).

H. v. 'Aureomaculata'   Strong broadly oval green leaves with yellow centres. Increase by division of the rootstock during early spring. 90 cm (3 ft).
H. v. 'Variegata'   Large green leaves with a bold creamy yellow margin. Increase by division of the rootstock during early spring. 90 cm (3 ft).

Iris aurea
A tall-growing iris with beautifully formed blossoms of intense golden yellow during summer. A very adaptable plant with bold sword-like green leaves. Easily increased by division immediately after flowering or seed sown as soon as ripe or in early spring. 1.2 m (4 ft).

Iris bulleyana
A lovely little Chinese iris with blue flowers produced during the first part of the summer. Bold tufts of grassy foliage. Can be propagated by division immediately after flowering or raised from seed sown immediately it ripens or during early spring. 60–75 cm (2–2½ ft).

Iris chrysographes
Narrow sword-shaped green foliage from which arise strong short stems with blossoms of rich velvety purple. Can be raised from seed, but the results are variable. Best lifted and divided after flowering. 60 cm (2 ft).

Iris kaempferi (Japanese clematis-flowered iris)
A beautiful swamp iris with tufts of broad grassy foliage and rich broad blossoms of deep purple during midsummer. Propagation is from seed sown during the spring or division of established clumps immediately after flowering. Propagation of cultivars is by division only. Must have an acid soil. 60–75 cm (2–2½ ft).
I. k. 'Blue Heaven'   Rich purple-blue velvety petals marked with yellow. 60–75 cm (2–2½ ft).
I. k. 'Landscape At Dawn'   Fully double, pale rose-lavender. 60–75 cm (2–2½ ft).
I. k. 'Mandarin'   A lovely deep violet-coloured cultivar with blossoms that look rather like those of a clematis. 60–75 cm (2–2½ ft).
I. k. 'Tokyo'   This is not a straight cultivar, but a mixed strain which is raised from seed. Many different colours and colour combinations. Easily raised from a spring sowing of seed. Good colours can be selected and reproduced by division immediately after flowering. 60–75 cm (2–2½ ft).
I. k. 'Variegata'   Of neat habit, this iris has lovely cream and green striped foliage and rather small violet-blue flowers during summer. 60 cm (2 ft).

Iris ochroleuca
A big bold yellow and white flowered species for almost any wet spot. Flowers appear during summer among tall glaucous sword-like leaves. Can be increased

Iris kaempferi 'Wada', an excellent moisture-loving iris.

from seed sown immediately it ripens or else in the early spring. Division of established clumps immediately after flowering. 1.5 m (5 ft).

Iris sibirica (Siberian iris)
This is a versatile blue-flowered iris that is now rarely grown as a species because of the wealth of cultivars that are about. *I. sibirica* has strong tufts of grassy foliage and erect stems of elegant pale blue flowers. Easily raised from seed, but flower colour will be variable. Good selections and cultivars like those below can be lifted and divided immediately after flowering or in early spring as the young spears of growth appear. 90 cm (3 ft).
I. s. 'Emperor' Deep violet-purple. 90 cm (3 ft).
I. s. 'Ottawa' Another deep violet cultivar which is widely grown. 90 cm (3 ft).
I. s. 'Perry's Blue' This is the sky blue cultivar that has largely replaced the ordinary species. 90 cm (3 ft).
I. s. 'Perry's Pygmy' One of the finest small-growing irises for the waterside. Deep violet blossoms. 45 cm (18 in).

Ligularia clivorum
A most attractive member of the daisy family, with large violet-green heart-shaped leaves and huge mop heads of droopy orange flowers during late summer. Increase by division of the rootstock during the dormant period. 90–120 cm (3–4 ft).
L. c. 'Golden Queen' Golden yellow mop heads of flowers in late summer. Green heart-shaped leaves. Increase by division of the rootstock in winter. 90–120 cm (3–4 ft).
L. c. 'Orange Princess' A superb orange-flowered cultivar. The leaves are green with a purplish infusion. Increase by division of the rootstock when dormant. 90–120 cm (3–4 ft).

Ligularia stenocephala 'The Rocket'
Soaring wands of bright yellow daisy-like flowers during late summer. Big bold clumps of more or less triangular, coarsely toothed foliage. Increase by division of the rootstock during the dormant period. 1.5–2 m (5–6½ ft).

Ligularia veitchianus
Coarse green, almost triangular leaves and tall spires of yellow daisy-like flowers. These are produced in profusion during late summer and early autumn. Increase by division of the rootstock during the dormant period. 1–2 m (3½–6½ ft).

Lobelia cardinalis (Cardinal flower)
An upright plant with bright green foliage and spires of vivid red flowers. This is often confused with the purple-leaved *L. fulgens* which in nurseries is often sold as *L. cardinalis*. This is a perennial lobelia, but one which does appreciate a little

winter protection. Lift one or two overwintering rosettes and place them in a frame or unheated greenhouse for safe-keeping. In very cold areas a protective layer of straw or bracken during the winter is beneficial. Can be increased by dividing up the rosettes of overwintered foliage, from stem cuttings in the spring or else seed sown at the same period. 60–90 cm (2–3 ft).

Lobelia fulgens
Beetroot-coloured stems and leaves, together with spikes of bright red blossoms during summer. Can be increased by division during the spring, stem cuttings at the same time or seed sown before early summer. 60–90 cm (2–3 ft).

Lobelia 'Huntsman'
Brilliant scarlet flowers and green foliage. Late summer. Increased by division of overwintered rosettes in the spring. 60–90 cm (2–3 ft).

Lobelia 'Queen Victoria'
Maroon foliage and bright red flowers during late summer. Increased by division of overwintered rosettes in the spring. 60–90 cm (2–3 ft).

Lobelia syphilitica
Green foliage and spires of blue, or occasionally white flowers during late summer. Easily raised from seed sown during spring under glass. 60–90 cm (2–3 ft).

Lobelia × vedrariensis
Mid-green foliage flushed and infused with purple. Flowers of intense violet are produced during late summer and early autumn. Easily raised from a spring sowing of seed under glass or division of overwintered rosettes in early spring. 75–90 cm (2½–3 ft).

Lysimachia nummularia (Creeping Jenny)
This is a more or less evergreen carpeting plant that is ideal for disguising the edges of a pool and bog garden. It also provides attractive ground cover between taller growing plants in marshy areas. During summer the fresh green foliage becomes studded with starry buttercup-like blossoms. Easily increased from short stem cuttings taken at any time during the growing season. 5 cm (2 in).

L. n. 'Aurea' The most wonderful golden-leaved creeping plant. All the virtues of the common species, but the added bonus of brightly coloured foliage. Easily increased from short stem cuttings taken during the growing period. 5 cm (2 in).

Lysimachia punctata
An upright plant with downy foliage and spikes of bright yellow flowers rather like those of the creeping Jenny. Increased by division of the rootstock during the dormant period. 60–90 cm (2–3 ft).

Lythrum salicaria (Purple loosestrife)

For mid to late summer flowering few moisture-loving garden plants can surpass the loosestrife for colour and reliability. The common species has a bushy upright habit and produces myriad slender spires of deep rose-purple blossoms. Easily increased by division during the dormant period. 1.2 m (4 ft).

L. s. 'Brilliant'   A very fine pink-flowered sort. Increase by division during the dormant period. 90 cm–120 cm (3–4 ft).

L. s. 'Lady Sackville'   Strong rose pink selection. A plant of excellent habit. Increase by division during the dormant period. 90 cm–120 cm (3–4 ft).

L. s. 'Robert'   Another soft pink cultivar of exceptional merit. Increase by division during the dormant period. 90–120 cm (3–4 ft).

Lythrum virgatum

Shorter spires of purple blossom and dark green foliage. Increase by division of the rootstock during the dormant period. 45 cm (18 in).

L. v. 'Dropmore Purple'   Deep purple flowers during mid to late summer. Increase by division during the dormant period. 45 cm (18 in).

Mimulus cardinalis (Cardinal monkey flower)

A plant for damp conditions rather than really wet. Attractive hoary foliage and brilliant scarlet-orange flowers during late summer. Not always hardy in cold areas. Easily overwintered as rooted cuttings taken during late summer, in a cold greenhouse or frame. Seed sown during early spring in a propagator provides an alternative method of propagation. 45–60 cm (1½–2 ft).

Mimulus 'Highland Pink'

This is a pink-flowered version of *M.* 'Highland Red'. 15 cm (6 in).

Mimulus 'Highland Red'

Short-growing, with soft green foliage and bright red blooms throughout the summer. Increase by spring division of overwintered rosettes. 15 cm (6 in).

Mimulus 'Hose-in-Hose'

Bright yellow-flowered variety in which each bloom has another inside, almost like a double flower. Increase by spring division of overwintered rosettes. 20–30 cm (8–12 in).

Mimulus lewisii

Closely allied to *M. cardinalis* and requiring the same method of overwintering as short, rooted stem cuttings. Hoary foliage and lovely rose-lilac blossoms throughout the summer. 30–45 cm (12–18 in).

Mimulus 'Monarch Strain'

One of the very best free-flowering, mixed coloured, seed-raised strains of the monkey flower. Gorgeous exotic-looking blooms throughout the summer. Not reliably perennial and best raised from seed sown under glass early in the spring. 20–30 cm (8–12 in).

Mimulus 'Whitecroft Scarlet'
One of the tiniest of bog garden plants. Dense carpets of fresh green foliage and masses of brilliant scarlet blossoms. Often does not survive the winter intact in cold areas, where patches of foliage die out. Easily raised from seed sown under glass during early spring. Flowers all summer long, even from a sowing during the same year. 10 cm (4 in).

Peltiphyllum peltatum (Umbrella plant)
Stout stems bear immense leaves of bronzy green, often 30 cm (12 in) in diameter. They are handsomely lobed and toothed and preceded in spring by globular heads of rose-coloured blossoms on sturdy stems 45 cm (18 in) high. Easily increased by division of the fleshy rhizome during early spring. 45–90 cm.

Petasites japonicus (Butterbur)
This is only suitable where plenty of space is available, for it produces large unwieldy cabbage-like foliage during the summer. It is a welcome harbinger of spring, producing crowded heads of white flowers on neat short stems scarcely before the winter has passed. 1.5 m (4 ft).

Phormium tenax (New Zealand flax)
Not usually associated with the bog garden nowadays, but nevertheless a plant of wet places. This species is sometimes used as a poolside or waterside plant, especially in a formal setting where its bold sword-like leaves add an architectural quality. The foliage is a metallic bronze-green and from among it is sometimes produced an odd-looking flower stem with curious reddish and ochre flowers. It is readily raised from seed, the young plants being grown on in pots. Old plants can sometimes be divided successfully in the spring. 90 cm–150 cm (3–5 ft).

P. t. 'Atropurpurea' Attractive reddish-purple foliage. Variable when reproduced from seed. Careful division of good coloured plants is best. 90–120 cm (3–4 ft).

P. t. 'Variegata' Strongly variegated foliage of green, yellow and white. Less vigorous than the preceding. 75–90 cm (2½–3 ft).

The following are *Phormium* hybrids:

P. 'Cream Delight' Foliage vivid creamy-yellow banded with green. Increased by careful division in the spring. 75–90 cm (2½–3 ft).

P. 'Dark Delight' Leaves of deep maroon. Increased by careful division in the spring. 75–90 cm (2½–3 ft).

P. 'Emerald Green' A plain green foliage cultivar. Increased by careful division in the spring. 75 cm (2½ ft).

P. 'Maori Maiden' Extraordinary foliage of red, pink and brown. Increased by careful division. 45–60 cm (1½–2 ft).

Primula alpicola (Moonlight primula)

Early summer-flowering hardy perennial with pendant bell-shaped flowers varying in colour from yellow to white and purple, carried on slender flower stems. Leaves small, rounded and bright green. A plant for a cool moist position in the less waterlogged part of the bog garden. Propagation by early spring division or seed, preferably sown shortly after harvesting. 15–60 cm (6 in–2 ft).

P. a. alba   A pure white-flowered form that comes almost 100% true from seed. 15–60 cm (6 in–2 ft).

P. a. luna   A beautiful sulphurous-yellow-flowered form. Like its white counterpart this comes almost completely true from seed. 15–60 cm (6 in–2 ft).

P. a. violacea   A purple to violet selection which is fairly erratic from seed. To ensure plants of even stature and colour this should be propagated by division in early spring, just as the young shoots are emerging. 15–60 cm (6 in–2 ft).

Primula anisodora

A plant with strongly aromatic flowers and foliage. Flowers brownish purple with a green eye and borne in small tiered whorls around a strong flower stalk during summer. Leaves large, green, more or less oval, and rather coarse. A reliable perennial well suited to a moist position in either sun or shade. Easily increased from seed, especially if sown immediately after harvesting. Plants can be carefully divided during early spring or immediately after flowering. 30–60 cm (1–2 ft).

Primula aurantiaca

Hardy perennial primula with bright reddish orange flowers in early summer arranged in neat tiered whorls. Leaves green, long, broad and rather coarse, slightly aromatic. A reliable plant for bog garden or waterside. Revels in a richly organic damp medium. Increase from seed, preferably sown immediately after harvesting. Packeted seed sown the following year usually germinates in an erratic fashion. Established plants can be divided as they emerge through the soil during early spring or immediately they finish flowering. 60–90 cm (2–3 ft).

Primula beesiana

A vigorous hardy perennial flowering in early summer. Flowers of rosy carmine with a yellow eye are borne in dense tiered whorls on stout flower stalks. Leaves large, green, cabbagey, up to 30 cm (12 in) long. An excellent strong-growing plant for the bog garden or poolside. Enjoys a cool deep root-run in a richly organic damp soil. Grows well in either sun or partial shade. Increase by division of the emerging crowns in spring, or else from seed sown immediately after harvesting. Packeted seed sown during the spring usually germinates, but somewhat erratically. 60–75 cm (2–2½ ft).

Primula bulleyana

A hardy perennial primula that flowers during early summer. Large deep orange flowers arranged in tiered whorls on strong flower stalks. Leaves, large, green and cabbagey. Must have a cool damp root-run in a deep richly organic soil. Grows well in sun or partial shade. Can be propagated by careful division in the early spring just as the shoots are emerging, or immediately after flowering. Freshly gathered seed germinates freely. Packeted seed sown the following spring germinates in an erratic manner. 60–90 cm (2–3 ft)

Primula burmanica

Vigorous hardy perennial primula flowering during early summer. Large reddish purple blossoms with conspicuous yellow eyes are borne in tiered whorls on strong flower stems. Leaves green, large and cabbagey. Must have a good damp, deep, cool soil rich in organic matter. Will grow successfully in sun or shade. Propagate from careful division of the crowns during early spring just as they are coming into growth, or immediately after flowering. Seed that has been freshly gathered germinates freely if sown immediately. 60 cm (2 ft).

Primula capitata

Hardy perennial mid to late summer with small deep violet bell-shaped flowers arranged in rounded flattened heads on short, stout flower stems. The small rosettes of lance-shaped green leaves are covered generously in white meal, especially beneath, as are the flower stems. A lovely plant for a damp, but not waterlogged position. Does not divide easily, plants tending to be individuals which grow larger without producing offsets. Easily raised from seed, especially when freshly gathered and sown straight away. 15–30 cm (6–12 in).

P. c. mooreana   Very similar to the species and flowering over a slightly later period. Flowers open in a more flattened head, leaves green above, with a dense white meal beneath. 15–30 cm (6–12 in).

P. c. sphaerocephala   Funnel-shaped deep violet flowers in tight rounded heads during mid and late summer. Leaves lance-shaped, green above and beneath. 15–30 cm (6–12 in).

Primula chungensis

A lovely hardy perennial primula with handsome tiered whorls of pale orange blossoms during early summer. Leaves, green, coarse, and rather cabbagey form in large clumps. Revels in a moist richly organic soil in full sun or partial shade. Readily increased from seed sown as soon as possible after harvesting. Older seed will germinate, but maybe somewhat erratic. 60–75 cm (2–2½ ft).

Primula cortusoides

Spring-flowering hardy, but often short-lived perennial. Flowers small, purplish rose in many flowered umbels. Leaves rounded soft green and downy. A very easily grown plant for a damp shady spot but not suited to really wet conditions. Plants grow well for two or three years, but then start to deteriorate and often die out. Replace regularly from seed which germinates reasonably freely at any time. 15–30 cm (6–12 in).

Primula denticulata (Drumstick primula)

Very popular, vigorous spring flowering perennials for the bog garden. Large heads of lilac, pink or purplish blossoms crowded into globular heads on strong flower stalks during early spring. Leaves long, broad and coarse, often dusted with a white or yellowish meal. Flower stems often coated as well. Completely hardy and easily increased from seed sown during the spring or early summer, seedlings flowering during their second year. Good forms can be reproduced from root cuttings taken during the dormant period. 30–60 cm (1–2 ft).

P. d. var. alba (White drumstick primula)   Similar in almost every respect to P. denticulata, except producing heads of pure white flowers. Extremely variable when raised from seed, some occasional purplish or lilac-flowered forms appearing. The vigour of the plants and density of the globular flower head are very variable with seed-raised plants. The most reliable method of reproduction is root cuttings of selected forms. 30–60 cm (1–2 ft).

P. d. var. cachmiriana   A vigorous variety of P. denticulata with fairly consistent purple blooms. This is generally more robust than the ordinary species, with flowerheads that are slightly larger, and bold cabbagey foliage coated beneath with yellow meal. Most plants are grown from seed, but any particularly fine forms can be propagated from root cuttings during the dormant period. 30–60 cm (1–2 ft).

P. d. 'Rosea'   A rich crimson form identical to P. denticulata, except in colour. Best increased from root cuttings during the dormant period. 30–60 cm (1–2 ft).

Primula florindae (Himalayan cowslip)

A giant primula which flowers from midsummer into early autumn. Large heads of pendant sulphur yellow blooms above broad, coarse green leaves. Perfectly hardy and reliably perennial. A lovely streamside plant fully tolerant of the rising and falling of the water. Enjoys a deep cool soil with plenty of organic matter incorporated into it. Propagates freely from seed sown at any time during the spring or summer. Plants can be divided during early autumn when flowering is over. 60–90 cm (2–3 ft).

P. f. 'Art Shades'   This is a seed-raised selection in which the flowers vary from the palest primrose and apricot to burnt orange. Handsome plants for adding colour variation during late summer. Although popularly seed-raised, exceptionally fine colour forms can be reliably increased by division immediately after flowering. 60–90 cm (2–3 ft).

Primula denticulata, the drumstick primula is one of the earliest spring–flowering moisture lovers.

Primula 'Harlow Car Hybrids'

This is probably the best known strain of candelabra primulas ever developed. Flowering from early spring into summer they embrace almost every colour imaginable. Propagation is by seed sown immediately after harvesting or else in spring. This yields a good strong mixture of colours. Especially fine colours that appear can be reproduced by careful division in early spring as the shoots start to appear or immediately after flowering. 60–75 cm (2–2½ ft).

Primula helodoxa

Hardy summer-flowering perennial primula with vivid yellow, open bell-shaped flowers in tiered whorls. Leaves bright green, long and tapering. While enjoying dampness, it will not tolerate standing with its roots in water. Easily increased from freshly gathered seed sown immediately. Packeted seed retains little viability and relatively few seedlings are produced from its erratic germination. Division of the clumps in early spring just as they are coming into growth is satisfactory. So is lifting and dividing immediately after flowering. 60–90 cm (2–3 ft).

Primula heucherifolia

Spring-flowering hardy perennial with small mauve-pink to deep purple blossoms in many-flowered umbels. Leaves rounded and lobed, coarse and sparsely hairy. An easy plant for a damp spot. Benefits from a little shade. Readily increased from seed, the old plants periodically being replaced as they deteriorate rather quickly with age. 15–30 cm (6–12 in).

Primula 'Inverewe'

The most spectacular candelabra primula. An early summer-flowering perennial with bright orange flowers in dense tiered whorls. The flower stems are heavily coated with white meal and contrast beautifully with the vivid blossoms. Leaves plain green, rather coarse, more or less elliptical and rather cabbagey. Demands a good richly organic soil and constant moisture. As it does not set seed it must be divided either in early spring as shoots are just starting to push through the soil, or else immediately flowering is over. 45–75 cm (1½–2½ ft).

Primula japonica

A strong-growing hardy perennial primula with bold flowers of deep red produced in tiered whorls on extremely stout flower stalks during late spring and early summer. Large cabbage-like leaves, coarse, green with a slight bluish tint. Demands a damp richly organic soil. Easily increased from seed, even packeted seed producing tolerable results. Plants can also be divided during early spring, just as new shoots are emerging, or alternatively immediately flowering is over. 45–75 cm (1½–2½ ft).

P. j. 'Miller's Crimson' The finest form of P. japonica, the colour being particularly intense and uniform. In every other respect identical to the species.

Although a named cultivar this comes true from seed. Seed sown immediately after harvesting is best, but packeted seed also yields creditable results. Plants can of course be divided in early spring or immediately after flowering. 45–75 cm (1½–2½ ft).

P. j. 'Postford White'   This has flowers of cool icy white with a conspicuous orange-yellow central ring. Sometimes the flowers show a hint of pink. A vigorous plant, the same in most respects to *P. japonica*, but with somewhat paler foliage. Another primula that comes almost 100% true from seed. Freshly gathered seed produces the best results, but reasonable germination can be expected from packeted seed. Plants can be lifted and divided during early spring or immediately after flowering. 45–75 cm (1½–2½ ft).

Primula muscarioides

Mid summer flowering hardy perennial with many-flowered heads giving it a similar appearance to that spring-flowering bulb, the grape hyacinth (hence its name). The individual flowers are very different, of course, being tubular, pendant and a deep purplish blue. The leaves are rounded, dull green and slightly downy. Best grown in a damp spot with a little dappled shade rather than in the bog garden. Easily raised from seed sown as soon after harvesting as possible. Well established plants can be divided during early spring, as soon as signs of growth are detected. 30–45 cm (12–18 in).

Primula poissonii

An interesting hardy perennial primula flowering in early summer with tiered whorls of deep purplish-crimson flowers with yellow eyes. Leaves oblong or obovate, coarse, glaucous green in neat clumps. Requires a moist richly organic medium in sun or partial shade. Will not tolerate having its roots standing in water. Easily raised from seed, especially if it is sown directly after harvesting. Plants can be divided during early spring as shoots just start to appear or immediately following flowering. 30–45 cm (12–18 in).

Primula polyneura

Spring-flowering hardy perennial with pale rose, rich rose or purple blooms on slender flower stalks. Leaves more or less triangular, green and downy. A good subject for richly organic soil at the waterside. Easily increased from seed and best replaced every few years. 15–30 cm (6–12 in).

Primula pulverulenta

A great favourite among gardeners. Spring and early summer flowering with deep red blooms with conspicuous purple eyes. Bold tiered flower stems densely covered in white meal rise on green cabbagey leaves. Easily increased from seed. Readily divisible in spring when its shoots are just peeping through the soil, or alternatively in mid summer when flowering is over. 60–90 cm (2–3 ft).

P. p. 'Bartley Strain'   A fine pink-flowered strain that is the same in every other respect as ordinary *P. pulverulenta*. Easily raised from seed, although established plants can be divided in the spring as evidence of growth is seen. They can also be divided after flowering. 60–90 cm (2–3 ft).

Primula rosea
An early spring-flowering perennial for a wet place at the waterside. Beautiful glowing pink primrose-like blossoms appear among green leaves that are attractively flushed with copper or bronze. These spring tints are short-lived, the broadly lance-shaped leaves soon reverting to plain green. Easily increased from seed, ideally sown directly it ripens. The plants produced in this manner are sometimes variable in both colour and stature so selection of the best forms for propagation by division is desirable. Division should be undertaken immediately after flowering. 10–15 cm (4–6 in).

P. r. 'Delight'   A lovely cultivar with brilliant rose pink blooms, superior in both quality and size to the species. Must be increased by division. 10–15 cm (4–6 in).

P. r. 'Grandiflora'   A larger-flowered form with similar rose pink blooms and plain green leaves that have a hint of bronze in the spring. Not as consistent as 'Delight', because the plants commonly offered in garden centres are usually seed-raised. The true 'Grandiflora' is increased by division to maintain consistency. When a group of 'Grandiflora' is in flower it is wise to mark the best ones and reproduce those by division. 10–15 cm (4–6 in).

Primula saxatilis
Short-lived perennial with many-flowered umbels of rosy violet or pinkish mauve appearing in spring and early summer. Rounded, toothed and lobed leaves with long leaf stalks, green, soft and downy. An easy plant for a shady spot in a richly damp organic soil rather than a true bog. Plants start to deteriorate after a couple of years and need replacing. Easily raised from seed sown during the spring or summer. 10–30 cm (4–12 in).

Primula secundiflora
A charming hardy summer-flowering perennial with reddish purple, pendant, funnel-shaped blooms borne in groups on slender flower stems. Leaves lance-shaped, green, often with a yellowish meal beneath in the spring. Enjoys a little dappled shade and a cool, moist root run. Well suited to the bog garden but will not enjoy sitting in water during the winter. Easily increased from seed sown directly after harvesting, or by division of established plants in the early spring. 30–45 cm (1–1½ ft).

Primula sieboldii
Early summer-flowering perennial primula with umbels of rounded white, pink or purple blooms with conspicuous eyes. Leaves rounded and toothed, soft green and finely downy. Gorgeous plants for a shady spot in moist soil rather than

Primula pulverulenta grows in any moist soil in sun or shade.

a bog. Easily increased from seed or, in the case of named cultivars, by careful division in early spring or directly after flowering. In years gone by there were many cultivars available. These have gone into decline and only a few old favourites like 'Wine Lady' are popularly available. 15–20 cm (6–8 in).

Primula sikkimensis

Hardy summer-flowering perennial with soft yellow, pendant, funnel-shaped flowers on slender stems. Leaves coarse, green, rounded and shiny. A bog plant that revels in wet soils with a high organic matter content, preferably in partial shade. Easily increased from division of established plants after flowering. Seed sown during spring or early summer is usually quite successful, even if it has been packeted the previous year. 45–75 cm (1½–2½ ft).

Primula sinoplantaginea

Late spring-flowering, short-lived, hardy perennial. Deep purple, fragrant tubular blossoms in small umbels. Leaves narrow, lance-shaped, smooth green with yellowish farina beneath. Established plants do not divide well, but seed is set freely and young plants are easily raised, especially if the seed can be sown fresh. A plant for a damp but not wet spot at the waterside. 15–20 cm (6–8 in).

Primula sinopurpurea

A delightful hardy perennial primula flowering in spring. Gorgeous violet-purple tubular blooms in six to twelve flowered umbels. Broadly lance-shaped, plain green leaves with serrated edges, sparingly covered with meal beneath. A more reliable and vigorous plant than *P. sinoplantaginea*, but of the same general aspect. Excellent for waterside planting. Readily raised from seed, especially if sown shortly after harvesting. Spring division is possible, but needs great care to ensure a reasonable percentage re-establishment. 30–45 cm (12–18 in).

Primula vialii (Orchid primula)

Late spring or early summer-flowering hardy perennial, although some gardeners suggest that it is monocarpic and dies after flowering. One of the most bizarre primulas, sporting short flower spikes that look rather like miniature red hot pokers, being dense heads of small tubular flowers of red and bluish purple. Small lance-shaped, soft, downy green leaves. Suitable for a damp but not waterlogged spot in the bog garden. Easily raised from seed, preferably sown shortly after collection. Lifting and dividing plants is largely futile as almost half of them are likely to be lost during the operation. A regular supply of young seed raised plants should always be maintained to counter the plant's habit of fading out after flowering. 30–45 cm (12–18 in).

Primula waltoni

Hardy perennial with deep wine-purple, occasionally pink flowers in late spring or early summer. Neat heads on strong wiry stems. Leaves lance-shaped, but rounded, bright green. A good plant for a damp, but not waterlogged spot. Appreciates dappled shade. Does not always divide freely, but is very easily raised from seed, especially that which has been freshly gathered. 30–45 cm (12–18 in).

Primula yargongensis

Late spring-flowering hardy perennial primula for a damp corner, but not a waterlogged spot. Flowers tubular, bell-shaped, mauve, pink or purple with a white or cream eye in small umbels. Leaves rounded or elliptical plain green. An ideal plant for the waterside. Benefits from a very damp, richly organic soil, but will rot off if forced to sit in permanent moisture. Easily raised from seed sown immediately after it ripens. Plants set seed freely providing that they receive constant moisture. 10–30 cm (4–12 in).

Rheum palmatum (Ornamental rhubarb)

Although a number of rheums are grown in gardens this is the most reliable for the bog garden. It has broad spreading foliage and spikes of small decorative creamy white blossoms. It is best propagated by division of the crowns during the spring just as they are breaking into growth. Seed-raised plants are very variable. 1.5–1.8 m (5–6 ft).

R. p. var. *tanguticum* The foliage of this form usually has a purplish cast and is always deeply cut. The flowers should be pink or rose-purple, but sometimes plants yield white blooms. The best forms should be propagated by division during the early spring. Seed raising cannot be recommended. 1.5–1.8 m (5–6 ft).

R. p. 'Bowles Crimson' This is almost identical to the species, but has foliage with a strong purplish red infusion and crimson flower spikes. This must be propagated from spring division of the crowns. Seed raised plants are totally unreliable from the point of view of colour or form. 1.5–1.8 m (5–6 ft).

Rodgersia tabularis

One of the most suitable rodgersias for the bog garden. Pale green circular leaves and dense panicles of creamy white flowers during summer. Easily increased by division of established crowns during early spring, or seed sown under glass at the same period. 90–120 cm (3–4 ft).

Salix alba 'Chermesina' (Scarlet willow)

If grown on a stooling system as recommended for cornus, this becomes a most useful shrub for winter colour. Brilliant orange-scarlet stems are produced if they are cut hard back each spring. This also maintains a manageable shrubby plant. Propagate from hardwood cuttings during the winter. 1.2–1.5 m (4–5 ft) if stooled annually.

S. a. 'Vitellina' (Golden willow)

If this is treated in the same way as *S.a.* 'Chermesina' the reward will be brilliant yellow winter stems. Cut back each spring. Increase from hardwood cuttings taken during the winter. 1.2–1.5 m (4–5 ft) if stooled annually.

Salix daphnoides (Violet willow)
If cut back hard as recommended for the other willows this will yield the most lovely violet winter stems. Propagate from hardwood cuttings during the winter. 1.2–1.5 m (4–5 ft) if stooled annually.

Schizostylis coccinea (Kaffir lily)
An attractive streamside plant that flowers during the autumn with bright red flowers among grassy foliage rather like a small day lily or *Hemerocallis*. Easily propagated by division during early spring. 30–60 cm (1–2 ft).
S. c. 'Grandiflora'   The same as the ordinary Kaffir lily, but with much larger flowers. Increased by division during early spring. 30–60 cm (1–2 ft).
S. c. 'Mrs Hegarty'   A rose-pink cultivar with elegant slender stems of blossoms. Propagation by division during early spring. 30–60 cm (1–2 ft).

Symplocarpus foetidus (Skunk cabbage)
A curious bog plant with quaintly hooded arum-like flowers of purple and green. These appear before its large, bright green cabbagey foliage. Propagation by division during early spring before the flowers appear. 75–90 cm (2½–3 ft).

Taxodium distichum (Swamp cypress)
This can only be recommended for the larger bog garden. A very fine deciduous conifer of pyramidal habit. Pale green summer foliage turns russet as autumn approaches. When well established in really wet conditions produces strange knobbly breathing roots or 'knees'. Can be propagated from summer cuttings or seed sown during spring or early summer. 20 m (65 ft).

Trollius asiaticus
Deep yellow buttercup-like flowers on strong wiry stems above compact mounds of finely toothed, bronze-green leaves. Spring and early summer flowering. Propagate by seed sown in spring or else division of established crowns during the dormant period. 30–45 cm (12–18 in).

Trollius chinensis
Beautiful yellow globular flowers are produced above hummocks of round or kidney-shaped leaves during spring and early summer. Propagate by seed sown in spring or else division of established crowns during the dormant period. 30–45 cm (12–18 in).

Trollius × cultorum 'Earliest of All'
The most popular of all the trollius or globe flowers. Rich canary yellow, almost globular flowers on strong wiry stems during spring and early summer. Handsome rounded toothed foliage. Increase by division during the dormant period. 30–45 cm (12–18 in).

The bold architectural foliage of this ornamental rhubarb adds a touch of the tropical.

T. × c. **'Fireglobe'**   A reddish orange flowered cultivar of exceptional merit. Increase only by division of the rootstock during the dormant period. 30–45 cm (12–18 in).

T. × c. **'Golden Queen'**   A well-tried cultivar with golden yellow blossoms during spring and early summer. Bright green toothed foliage. Increase by division of the rootstock during the dormant period. 30–45 cm (12–18 in).

T. × c. **'Orange Globe'**   The finest orange-flowered trollius. Blooms during spring and early summer. Leaves dark green and toothed. Increase by division of the rootstock during the dormant period. 30–45 cm (12–18 in).

Trollius europaeus (Common globe flower)

A lovely species with lemon yellow globular blooms that appear during spring and early summer. Compact mounds of bright green lobed foliage. Propagate from seed sown during the spring or division of the rootstock during the dormant period. 30–60 cm (1–2 ft).

Trollius yunnanensis

Bright yellow, cup-shaped or almost flat flowers during late spring on strong wiry stems. Basal clusters of rather irregular or oval leaves. Propagate by seed sown during the spring or division of established plants during the dormant period. 60 cm (2 ft).

Vaccinium angustifolium (Low bush blueberry)

A shrub of neat habit requiring a very wet acid soil. Pale green lance-shaped leaves which turn fiery red and orange in the autumn. The flowers are small, bell-shaped, white or red tinted and produced in abundance during late spring. Fruits blue-black, sweet and edible. Increased by cuttings taken during spring or autumn. 1.5 m (5 ft).

Vaccinium arboreum (Farkleberry)

A large deciduous shrub with leathery, glossy oval leaves that turn bright orange-red in the autumn. Flowers small, white and bell-shaped in spring. Fruits black and inedible. Increased by cuttings taken during spring or autumn. 1.5–3 m (5–10 ft).

Vaccinium corymbosum (Swamp blueberry)

A dense growing shrub with oval or lance-shaped leaves of bright green turning scarlet and bronze in the autumn. Flowers pale pink or white, and produced freely during late spring. Fruits large, black and edible. Increased by cuttings taken during spring or autumn. 90–150 cm (3–5 ft).

CHAPTER 5

MOISTURE-LOVING FERNS

Ferns are rather special additions to the bog garden or waterside, for they provide cool greenery of many hues and unique shapes and forms that make excellent contrasts for any brash flower colours. Some, like the royal ferns, are stately focal points, but the majority are carpeting varieties that create an excellent blending of land and water, slipping down the banks of pool or stream and colonizing the lower reaches. Do not neglect their spring attire either, for all moisture-loving ferns produce wonderful fiddle-heads or croziers as their foliage emerges, an added bonus so early in the year. Few spring scenes can compare with royal fern croziers pushing through a carpet of the blue-flowered Siberian squill, *Scilla sibirica*.

Dryoperis palustris (Marsh buckler fern)

An elegant creeping fern that enjoys spreading from moist soil into water at the pool or stream side. Upright pale green, much divided fronds persist well into the winter in their brown dried state. Propagated by division of the creeping rootstock during spring. 30 cm (12 in).

Matteucia struthiopteris (Ostrich feather fern)

Handsome bright green lacy fronds arranged in a shuttlecock fashion around a stout woody rootstock. The fertile fronds are half the length of the barren ones and produced from the centre of the shuttlecock during midsummer. A tough, but beautiful species which spreads by wiry underground rhizomes. 90 cm (3 ft).

Onoclea sensibilis (Sensitive fern)

A lovely fern for beside a stream, with erect flattened fronds which grow from a thick, black creeping rootstock. In spring they emerge with a rose pink flush, but pass to pale green as summer progresses. This species will grow in standing water as well as wet ground. Increase by division of the rootstock during spring. 45–60 cm (1½–2 ft).

Osmunda regalis (Royal fern)

A tall and stately fern with large leathery fronds which change colour from pale green in the spring, through darker greens to rich burnished bronze in the autumn. Can be propagated from spores sown immediately after gathering, but more usually by division of established crowns in spring. 1.2–1.8 m (4–6 ft).

O. r. 'Cristata'   A smaller version of the common royal fern, but with

Ferns fill awkward corners and provide a pleasing green foil at the waterside.

attractively tasselled and twisted fronds. Propagate by division only. Spore-raised plants are variable. 90–120 cm (3–4 ft).

O. r. 'Purpurescens'   Very similar to O. *regalis*, but with fronds that have a permanent purplish flush. Propagate by division in the spring. 1.2–1.8 m (4–6 ft).

O. r. 'Undulata'   Attractive crimped and crested mid-green fronds. Propagate by division of the crowns in spring. Spore-raised plants are unreliable and general yield inferior progeny. 90–120 cm (3–4 ft).

Woodwardia virginica (Virginian chain fern)

Broad olive green fronds of a soft felty texture grown from a stout creeping rhizome. A difficult fern to establish, but a lovely plant for the poolside or bog garden when in a situation to its liking. Easily propagated by division during the spring. 60 cm (2 ft).

CHAPTER 6

REEDS, RUSHES, SEDGES AND BAMBOOS

These are all essentially foliage plants which provide a generous foil for colourful bog garden and marginal subjects as well as contributing stature and unique architectural qualities. Reeds, rushes, and sedges are treated separately as they have greater adaptability to soil conditions and are generally much easier to establish. Bamboos are more particular and a little more tricky to deal with. However, they should not be ignored, for they can offer a tremendous amount to a bog garden or waterside feature, especially if a touch of the Orient is desired.

Most reeds, rushes and sedges are rather spreading and so careful placement is necessary. It is possible to restrict their exuberance by confining them to a container plunged into the ground, but unless they are well fed and regularly replanted, they deteriorate rapidly. The best results are achieved by selecting planting positions where they are unlikely to be a nuisance and where you can easily get at them if they start to get out of hand. All can be readily controlled if you keep an eye on them and attend to maintenance regularly.

REEDS, RUSHES AND SEDGES

All these depend upon very wet soil for their prosperity. A number are very happy in containers on the marginal shelves of garden pools, forming the link between the pool and the bog garden. All will grow freely in wet or very damp cultivated soil.

Carex pendula (Pendulous sedge)
This is one of the few true sedges worth cultivating. A very happy inhabitant of wet soil rather than standing water. A tall dignified plant, with broad green strap-like leaves and long drooping spikes of brownish green catkin-like flowers which appear during the summer and persist into early autumn. Can be increased by careful division during early spring, but much better results are usually obtained from sowing the seed immediatly after ripening. 90–120 cm (3–4 ft).

Carex riparia (Great pond sedge)
Only the uninformed would plant this vigorous marginal in their bog garden, but the cultivars derived from it are well-behaved and quite appealing. 30–75 cm (1–2½ ft).

C. r. 'Aurea' A charming tufted grassy perennial with bright golden foliage which illuminates the waterside throughout the summer. Insignificant brownish flower spikes are sprinkled among the foliage. Although often offered as a marginal plant for the pool, it much prefers boggy soil at the waterside. Propagation is by careful division of established clumps during early spring. 30–75 cm (1–2½ ft).

C. r. 'Variegata' Very similar to the golden-leaved form, but foliage is variegated green and white. Propagation is by careful division of established clumps during early spring. 30–75 cm (1–2½ ft).

Cyperus longus (Sweet galingale)
Fresh green grass foliage and terminal umbels of stiff spiky leaves which radiate from the stem like the ribs of an umbrella. Small, insignificant brownish flower spikes are sprinkled among the leaves of the umbrella-like heads. A good creeping foliage plant which is ideal for stabilizing banks of streams and eroded soil areas at the waterside. Strong scrambling rhizomes which can be cut into small lengths during early spring serve as a ready means of propagation. Large clumps can also be divided and seed germinates freely, especially that which has been freshly gathered. 90–120 cm (3–4 ft).

Cyperus vegetus
This plant looks like the indoor umbrella plant, but is much more compact, with spreading umbels of bright green foliage and dense tufted spikelets of reddish mahogany flowers during late summer. Easily increased from seed sown immediately after ripening or during the following spring. Established plants can be divided at any time during the growing period. 30–60 cm (1–2 ft).

Eriophorum angustifolium (Cotton grass)
This is the most frequently encountered and most easily cultivated of the popular cotton grasses. Like all eriophorums it must have acid conditions. Cotton-wool-like flowerheads are produced among the grassy foliage during early summer. Propagation is by division of established plants during the spring. 30–45 cm (12–18 in).

Eriophorum latifolium (Broad-leaved cotton grass)
A species of similar habit to the popular cotton grass, but with broader, darker foliage. Liberal quantities of cotton-wool-like flowerheads are produced throughout the summer months. Requires an acid soil. Propagation is by division of established plants during the spring. 30–45 cm (12–18 in).

Glyceria aquatica 'Variegata' (Variegated water grass)
A most handsome and vigorous perennial grass that grows in damp soil or in shallow water. An excellent plant for stabilizing eroded banks. Elegant green and cream foliage, which during spring has a strong red infusion. Spires of rather dull

A tastefully planted streamside with pleasing contrasts of flowers and foliage.

grassy flowerheads. These are best removed when they appear as they detract from the beauty of the plant and cause deterioration in the quality of its foliage. Easily increased by division of established clumps during spring. 60–120 cm.

Juncus effusus 'Spiralis' (Corkscrew rush)

One of the few rushes worthy of cultivation. Similar in appearance to the common soft rush, but the dark green needle-like leaves are twisted and contorted like a corkscrew. A bizarre addition to the waterside which is a talking point rather than a plant of great beauty. Must be propagated by division during the spring. Selection of suitable material for propagation is most important. Any portions of the plant showing straight 'needles' should be discarded. Only propagate the contorted portions. 30–45 cm (12–18 in).

J. e. 'Vittatus' An old and well-loved rush sometimes listed under the name 'Aureostriatus'. A handsome gold and green variegated rush with straight needle-like leaves. Remove any green shoots immediately they are seen. Propagation is by division of the variegated portions during early spring. 30–45 cm (12–18 in).

Phragmites australis (Spire reed)

A fast-growing and very common reed which needs introducing with great care to small areas as it can become invasive if not carefully checked. Of bamboo-like appearance, it has handsome silvery white or purplish silky flowerheads, and althouth it is possible to cultivate it in a restricted area, it is essentially a plant of wide open spaces, looking best around the perimeter of lakes. It can be readily increased by division, the woody runners, each with a shoot, being detached and planted where required. 1.2–1.5 m (4–5 ft).

P. a. 'Variegatus' A much slower growing, shorter and more decorative plant than the preceding, with handsome cream and green striped foliage. Propagated by lifting and dividing established clumps during early spring. Only select material for replanting that is wholly variegated. 90–120 cm (3–4 ft).

Scirpus lacustris (Bulrush)

This is the true bulrush, the plant that allegedly cradled the infant Moses. The popular conception of a bulrush is in fact the brown poker-headed reedmace or *Typha*. *S. lacustris* is an extremely useful plant for shallow water or wet soil, producing stiff, dark green needle-like leaves from a short creeping rootstock. During late summer the foliage is bedecked with pendant tassels of crowded reddish-brown flowers. Propagation is by seed sown during the spring in pans of mud, or more usually by division of the creeping root system during spring, as soon as the plants start sprouting. 60–90 cm (2–3 ft).

Scirpus tabernaemontani (Glaucous bulrush)

Taller than the ordinary bulrush but with slender foliage of steel grey with a conspicuous mealy bloom. Propagation is by division of the creeping rootstock during spring as soon as the plants start sprouting. 90–150 cm (3–5 ft).

S. t. 'Albescens' Stout upright stems of glowing sulphurous white conspicuously marked with thin longitudinal stripes. These are produced from a thick creeping rootstock that is said not to be fully hardy in very cold districts. Propagation is by division of the creeping rootstock in spring just as the plants start to sprout. 90–120 cm (3–4 ft).

S. t. 'Zebrinus' (Zebra bush) A very popular mutant of *S. tabernaemontani*, with stems that are alternately barred white and green. When occasional plain green stems are produced these should be removed before they outgrow the more desirable variegated ones. The shortest of the bulrushes, this prefers to grow in really shallow water or mud. Propagation is by division of the creeping rootstock during spring just as the plants are starting to sprout. 90 cm (3 ft).

Sparganium erectum (Branched bur-reed)

A very resilient, rush-like plant which needs introducing with great caution as in circumstances to its liking it can become very invasive. It has branched stems with greenish bur-like beads and handsome narrow, bright green strap-like foliage. There is also a variety called *S. e.* var. *neglectum*, which differs mainly in its stem, which is red towards the base. Propagation is by seed or division during early spring. 45–90 cm (1½–3 ft).

Sparganium emersum (Unbranched bur-reed)

This is similar in every respect to the branched species, except that the unbranched stem gives a narrower, spire-like appearance to the flowerhead. Increases readily from seed or division during early spring. 45–90 cm (1½–3 ft).

Typha angustifolia (Narrow-leaved reedmace)

A tall-growing, elegant reedmace (often wrongly called 'bulrush'), with slender grey-green foliage and bold brown poker-like seed heads. A most elegant plant as a larger waterside feature. The fruiting heads are mature during early autumn and are often cut for indoor dry floral arrangements. Increase by division of the creeping rootstocks in the spring just as they start to sprout. 1–2 m (3½–6½ ft).

Typha latifolia (Great reedmace)

One of the most strikingly handsome hardy marginal aquatic plants, but also one of the most difficult to grow satisfactorily in the modern garden. A very vigorous plant which can easily become rampant. This is best enjoyed in the wild or when planted around a large expanse of water. A distinguished looking reed with broad, grey-green strap-like foliage and fat chocolate-coloured fruiting heads during late summer and early autumn. Increase by division of the creeping rootstock during spring as soon as growth commences. 1–2 m (3½–6½ ft).

T. l. 'Variegata' A lovely creamy and green variegated variety which can be safely introduced to the average poolside or bog garden. Not a vigorous grower. Increase from division of the rootstock during spring just as growth commences. 90–120 cm (3–4 ft).

Typha laxmanii
This is a well-proportioned reed with slender, willowy greyish green leaves and handsome brown fruiting heads. Not as invasive as its cousins, but nevertheless needs carefully watching. Increases readily by division of the creeping rootstock during early spring. 90–120 cm (3–4 ft).

Typha minima
The tiniest reedmace of all. A small plant with dark green grassy foliage and chunky, rounded, brown fruiting heads. Not at all invasive and very easy to grow. It does not possess the dignity of its more robust relatives, but it does mean that the gardener with limited space can still enjoy at least one member of this fascinating group of plants. Easily increased by division during early spring as the plants start into growth. 45 cm (18 in).

Zizania aquatica (Canadian wild rice)
An annual plant that is quite frequently offered for sale for the waterside. It is not intended as a decorative plant, its main purpose being to attract wildflowl and therefore more commonly used in wildlife or game ponds. Nevertheless it is a handsome grass with slender arching reed-like foliage. Increase from seed sown in trays of mud during early spring. Transplant the seedlings into very wet soil. 1.8–2.4 m (6–8 ft).

Zizania latifolia
A perennial species of more modest stature. Another inhabitant of the wildlife pool. Bold green grassy foliage, but rarely ever flowers in northern Europe. Increased from imported seed or more usually by division during early spring. 1.2–1.5 m (4–5 ft).

BAMBOOS

While a number of the plants just described have the general aspect of a bamboo, their behaviour and requirements are very different. Not that the true bamboos are particularly difficult to cultivate, it is just that they take a little more time and care than most plants to get going successfully.

Pot-grown bamboos are the easiest to establish. These should be knocked out of their pots and planted without disturbance during late spring or early summer. Clumps dug up from open ground lose most of their soil when being lifted and can be tricky to get going. However, if they do become established they provide more substantial plants much sooner.

A frequent problem during the initial stages of establishment is windrock. This is the moving of the stems and foliage by the wind which in turns disturbs the roots and prevents them from establishing quickly. This can be prevented by carefully reducing the height of the canes by about one third and tying the cut stems together, thus presenting a much narrower profile to the wind. The stems can be untied once the plants are well established. Watering is also vital for several months after planting if growth is to continue unchecked.

Apart from their importance as decorative subjects, bamboos have a secondary economic value which gardeners often overlook – the production of canes for staking. Not all bamboos are suitable for this purpose, but both *Arundinaria japonica* and *A. anceps* yield suitable canes. Mature green canes should be cut during the summer and spread out to dry in a cool airy shed until the following spring, when they will be ready for use.

As bamboos rarely flower or set seed, propagation is limited to division. On the occasions when bamboos do flower, the plants die afterwards, so this is not a welcome occurrence. Division of bamboos is best undertaken during the spring or early summer. Choose the young culms or shoots from the outer part of the plant, as this is strong and vigorous and likely to produce the best plants. The older central portion of a clump is unlikely to grow away strongly having been disturbed, indeed much of it will show few signs of life. All the bamboos described here like soil that is constantly moist, some tolerating very wet conditions indeed.

Arundinaria anceps
A popular kind usually found in older gardens. Tall brownish, cylindrical canes and coarse, pendant green foliage. 3–3.5 m (10–12 ft).

A. japonica (Metake)
Slim, elegant canes supporting large green leaves with greyish undersides. The most frequently encountered bamboo. 3–4 m (10–13 ft).

A. murieliae
Slender yellowish canes, rarely thicker than a pencil and delicate narrow green leaves. One of the loveliest small bamboos. 2.5–3.5 m (8–12 ft).

A. nitida
Slender deep purple canes and narrow pea-green leaves. A fine smaller bamboo. 2.5–3.5 m (8–12 ft).

A. pygmaea
A short-growing carpeting species with slender dwarf canes and refined green foliage. Excellent for ground cover. 25 cm (10 in).

A. simonii
Striking canes with a distinctive white bloom during their juvenile stage. Leaf colour varies from dull to dark green, individual leaves often being half green and half glabrous beneath. 3.5–4.5 m (12–15 ft).

A. viridistriata
Dark green canes splashed with purple support foliage that is irregularly barred with gold and green. Remove the previous season's growth each spring to ensure strong, brightly coloured growth. 1–2 m (3–6 ft).

Phyllostachys aurea
A graceful bamboo with green canes which turn a creamy yellow. Pale green to gold foliage. 2.5–3 m (8–10 ft).

P. viridi-glaucescens
Strong, slender canes which in their early life are green, but mellow to rich yellow and support sheaves of bright green leaves with glaucous undersides. 4–4.8 m (13–16 ft).

Sasa palmata
A fairly vigorous, large-leaved bamboo which grows into dense thickets. An ideal background plant with bright green canes and foliage. 2–2.5 m (6–8 ft).

S. tessellata
Glossy green leaves up to 60 cm (2 ft) long and as much as 15 m (6 in) wide, borne on slender stems which look rather fragile, but in reality are quite sturdy. 2 m (6 ft).

Shibataea kumasasa
A short-growing bamboo with canes of curious irregular and acutely angular growth. Bright green when young, but changing to dull brown. Dense sheaves of broad, lance-shaped green leaves. 50–75 cm (20–30 in).

CHAPTER 7

INCREASING YOUR PLANTS

Most gardeners like to raise a few plants of their own, either for fun or to give away to friends. When establishing a bog garden or waterside planting it also proves to be much more economical to grow your own, either from seed, cuttings or division, than buy them from a nursery. These options also enable the enthusiast to raise plants which are not readily available from the horticultural trade. While for many of us moisture-loving plants are unfamiliar, the techniques for reproducing them are not far removed from traditional methods, although there are one or two little tricks that can make the difference between success and failure, especially with those that we loosely refer to as marginal plants.

RAISING MOISTURE-LOVING PLANTS FROM SEED

Seed is the most frequent method of propagation for most bog plants. The named kinds often have to be increased by cuttings or division, but the majority of others are most easily and quickly grown from seed. Even though a number, like the primulas, germinate best when sown directly after collecting from the parent plant, most moisture-loving plants, unlike marginal subjects, have a reasonable period of viability and can be sown the following spring, or even in many cases during early summer when pressure upon greenhouse and frame space is less. It is not such a tricky process either, for although moisture-loving plants often grow in quite wet conditions they can be propagated in a regular seed compost. Indeed, it is preferable that they are. Never be tempted to use ordinary garden soil for seed raising, even if it looks all right, for it will be full of all kinds of pests and disease which can cause problems later on.

SUITABLE COMPOSTS

Seeds of moisture-loving plants, like those of all others, only have one purpose in life, and that is to germinate. So provide them with the best conditions possible. Seed is generally quite expensive, so do not skimp on the cost of a pan or tray full of compost. Plants reflect directly the medium in which they are growing. However, it is very important to be selective about the compost used. Proper seed composts have few nutrients in them and are a perfect medium for germination. This lack of nutrients ensures that the compost is unlikely to damage tender seedlings, and that the growth of moss and liverworts is impaired. Soil-based composts such as those of the John Innes formula are theoretically suitable for all plants, but quicker results and better initial plants can often be raised in a good soilless compost. An all-peat soilless compost needs treating with a little reserve, as it has large air pockets within it. Unless great care is taken to ensure a smooth, even surface, fine seed like that of primula or perennial lobelia can get lost in an air void on the surface. While all-peat composts are excellent for larger seeded plants such as irises and rheums, smaller seeds will make a better start in a soilless compost consisting of a mixture of peat and fine sand. It is always wise when selecting a seed compost to choose a well-known branded kind rather than attempt to mix your own. The ingredients of home-made compost can be very variable and the results unsatisfactory. The small extra cost involved in purchasing properly mixed, scientifically balanced compost is an excellent investment.

Pans and trays should be filled almost to the top with a suitable compost. If this is of the John Innes type, it should then be firmed down and tamped level. If it is a soilless mixture it should just be gently tapped level. Never firm soilless compost. This excludes all the air and causes problems for emerging seedlings. It is often difficult to wet as well, particularly if it has been allowed to dry out for an hour or two. If you run into this difficulty, adding a drop of washing-up liquid to the water sometimes enables moisture to penetrate the compost more effectively.

SOWING THE SEED

Irrespective of the compost being used it is important to firm the corners and the edges of the seed tray with the fingers and the centre part with a wooden board (Fig. 5). This prevents the otherwise inevitable sinking of the compost around the edge and the irritating prospect of all the seeds being washed to the sides where they will germinate in a congested mess. Seed compost should be watered from above prior to sowing. This is particularly useful for soilless composts, as it settles them down, the undulations being levelled with a pinch of compost before sowing takes place.

Sprinkle the seed thinly over the surface of the compost and scatter a fine layer of sifted compost over the top. Large seeds like irises, which can be handled individually, can be spaced out regularly so that the later pricking out process is minimized. A light covering of compost gently tamped and watered then completes the operation. The covering of all but very fine seeds with compost is a necessity, but should not be carried to extremes. A good general rule is to cover the seed by about its own depth with compost.

Very fine seeds, like those of primulas, lobelia and mimulus, look rather like pepper and are very difficult to handle. Their even distribution over the surface of the compost can be helped by mixing the seed initially with a little dry silver sand. If this is poured into the seed packet and then shaken up, the seed should become fairly evenly distributed through the sand. This can then be scattered with the seed. As well as acting as a carrier, the sand indicates the area over which the seed has been distributed. The tray or pan, once sown, can be stood in a bowl of water and moisture allowed to soak through. This is very useful for all moisture-loving subjects, for watering from above, even from a watering can with a fine rose attachment, can redistribute or disturb the seeds on the surface.

With rare exceptions, trays or pans of seeds of moisture-loving plants all benefit from being stood on a warm heating cable when this is available. Warm compost conditions promote rapid germination in the majority of seeds. In a cool greenhouse, the combination of a soil-warming cable and a sheet of glass over the pan or tray can create a very effective micro-climate. Similarly, a sheet of newspaper placed lightly over a seed tray will act as perfect insulation and still allow sufficient light to pass through. It is important both with the glass and the newspaper that each is removed immediately germination has taken place. Once the seedlings emerge, maximum light is vital to ensure that they develop into stocky plants.

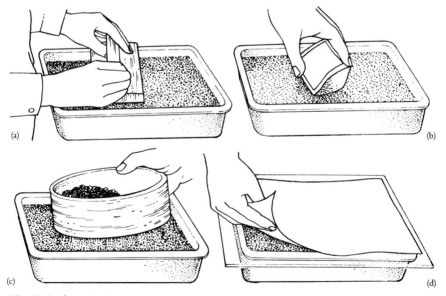

Fig. 5 *Seed sowing in trays*
(a) When using a soil-based compost, make it firm, so it does not sink unevenly later.
(b) Sprinkle seeds thinly and evenly over the level surface.
(c) Cover the seeds with a very thin layer of sieved compost or silver sand.
(d) Place a sheet of glass over the tray to retain moisture and cover with newspaper.

Harlow Car Hybrid primulas are the finest mixed strain for waterside planting.

DAMPING OFF

Some moisture-loving plants collapse shortly after germination with a disease called 'damping off'. This may seem odd as the plants are quite naturally moisture-lovers, but it is caused by a fungal disease which proliferates in the close atmosphere created by emerging seedlings that have been sown too thickly, or merely in very warm humid conditions. Certain varieties are more prone to this disease than others. Among the most likely to succumb are mimulus, lobelias and primulas. Prevention is better than cure, so immediately seedlings are seen to be actively growing a routine watering with Cheshunt compound is to be recommended. Once the seedlings have emerged, a modern fungicide with benomyl as the active ingredient can be used as an alternative, but as this only acts through the foliage the seedlings sometimes contract the disease before an application can be made. It is wise to repeat the treatment of either fungicide, but not both, every ten days until the plants are well established.

GROWING ON

When seedlings are large enough to handle they should be pricked out. This involves lifting and transplanting them into trays so that they can develop as individuals (Fig. 6). Most standard seed trays accommodate thirty-five plants, although some smaller growing plants like mimulus and lobelia can be planted at a greater density. Ideally the seedlings should have their seed leaves or cotyledons fully expanded and the first real leaves in evidence. Great care should be taken in handling the seedlings as they are very delicate and brittle. Never hold a seedling by its root or stem; always take hold of it by the seed leaf. Holding a tender seedling by the stem is likely to result in the appearance of a fungal disorder and the collapse of the plant. Plant the seedling slightly lower than it was in its original tray or pan; indeed in certain circumstances it can be planted so that the seed leaves are at compost level. This only applies if the seedling is short–jointed strong and healthy. Deep planting will rarely turn a drawn and etiolated seedling into a short healthy plant. If planted too deeply drawn seedlings will simply rot off and die.

If seedlings are pricked out into a potting compost they are unlikely to require feeding before being planted out or potted up. However, if planting or potting is delayed and the trays become full of roots it is useful to give a general liquid feed to maintain their vigour. Apart from this little special care is required during the development of the young plants providing that they have plenty of light, are watered regularly and an eye is kept open for pests and diseases. Apart from greenfly and mildew, few troubles are likely to be encountered in a well–organized greenhouse or frame. Both of these problems can be controlled by the use of systemic insecticides and fungicides.

The most important part of their cultivation, once they are successfully established in seed trays, is hardening off. This is the process by which the plants are weaned from the artificial environment of the greenhouse or window sill and prepared for the reality of life in the open garden. This even applies to plants that will be perfectly hardy, because they have been raised under very protected, favourable conditions. A cold frame is invaluable for this, for in chilly weather the frame light can remain on, whereas if the weather turns warm it can be removed entirely. What has to be achieved is a gradual transition over a period of two or three weeks. First of all the frame light is lifted to give ventilation. This is gradually increased until the light can be removed entirely during the day. It is then lifted slighly at night to allow ventilation. Eventually the light is removed both night and day.

If a frame is not available, and the plants have been raised on the window sill or in the sun lounge, the same effect can be provided by taking them out during the day and standing them in a sheltered place, returning them to the house for the night. This weaning process can continue in just the same way until the plants take on a hardy appearance. This is indicated by a stiffness of foliage, often associated with a darker green colour. If the plants have turned bluish-green, the weaning process has been too swift and the plants are checked. They will eventually grow out of it, but it does slow up their development, so gradual hardening off is vital.

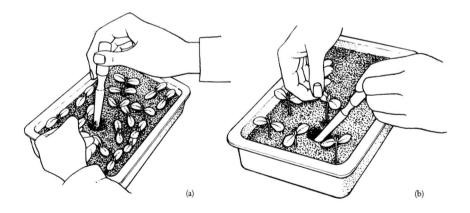

(a) (b)

Fig. 6 (a) Seedlings should be lifted as soon as large enough to handle, to reduce shock. (b) Space them out evenly in seed trays filled with potting compost.

POTTED PLANTS

While many plants like mimulus can be grown right up to the planting stage in trays, others are better grown on in pots. Indeed, primulas, trollius and even iris seem to make much better plants and transplant more readily when pot-grown. Soilless composts are light and easy to handle, with a good balance of nutrients, and young plants should advance quickly in all respects. It should be remembered though, that peat is an organic material that eventually decomposes, the process being hastened by regular feeding with liquid feeds. With peat forming the bulk of the compost, this decomposition can create problems if repotting is not regularly undertaken or the plants are not moved on into their permanent positions before deterioration sets in. Apart from the hostile airless conditions which develop in the medium and restrict proper root development, mosses and liverworts invade the surface and sciarid flies take up residence. These are irritating little insects, that although predominantly consumers of decomposing organic matter, will destroy vital nutrient-transmitting root hairs by their activities.

Soil-based composts on the other hand, while not producing such rapid growth, do provide more stability. Watering is easier to get right with a compost with a significant proportion of soil and this also acts as a buffer against the breakdown caused by any liquid feeding. The presence of soil in a compost allows for a greater margin of error when watering, for it permits the drainage of surplus moisture through the compost much more rapidly than if it were entirely of moisture-retaining peat. Indeed, it is the excessive moisture-holding capacity of peat, together with the relative difficulty of wetting it when it has been allowed to dry out, that makes soilless composts less popular with newcomers to plant raising. So use John Innes No. 1 potting compost for all actively growing plants, and if there is an option use clay pots. These are not any better for the plants, but it is well-known that the moisture content of the compost in a clay pot can be more easily recognized than when confined by a plastic pot. Take a short length of wood or a stick and tap the pot. If a dull thud results the compost is damp; if a ringing sound is heard, then it is dry. With the combination of John Innes compost and clay pots the gardener raising moisture-loving plants from seed should regularly meet with success.

RAISING MARGINAL PLANTS FROM SEED

The raising of marginal plants from seed is a little different from that advocated for other moisture-loving plants. Relatively few marginal subjects are increased this way, for almost all the fancy varieties do not come true from seed. There is unpredictability of germination too – some, like *Pontederia cordata*, only emerging freely when the seed is sown green, while others, such as *Alisma plantago-aquatica*, seem perfectly capable of germinating even when the seed is

The most exotic hardy primula, *Primula vialii*, revels in a damp border or peat garden.

12 months old.

The seeds of yet others, such as the skunk cabbage or lysichitons, are not even grain-like and free flowing. They are embodied in a thick sticky jelly and it is only while in this state that they are likely to germinate freely after sowing. When sowing seeds of this kind, sow all the jelly as well, taking care to spread the seeds out in it so that when they germinate the seedlings are not crowded.

Shallow pans should be filled with a good loam soil or standard aquatic planting medium and the seed distributed as evenly as possible over the surface. A light sprinkling of fine compost should cover the seeds and a gentle soaking from a watering can with a fine rose attachment will settle the compost. The pans should then be stood in a bowl with the water just at soil level and maintained at room temperature in a greenhouse or on the window ledge (Fig. 7).

It depends upon the variety being raised, but within a couple of weeks the seedlings will be seen emerging. When the first two or three true leaves are in evidence the plants should be pricked out. Lift them in clumps and wash them thoroughly to remove all the soil. Then gently tease them apart. A plastic seed tray or pan is the most useful container in which to prick out the seedlings, immersing it so that the compost is at the surface level of the water. They are then potted up and established (still standing in water) until large enough to plant out safely in the garden.

RAISING MOISTURE-LOVING PLANTS FROM STEM CUTTINGS

Many moisture-loving plants can be propagated with relative ease from stem cuttings. Even a number that are regularly raised from seed can be increased more rapidly from short spring stem cuttings, but these are mostly species. Named varieties rarely come true from seed and this is where cuttings really come into their own. It is also invaluable for plants like *Mimulus lewisii* and *M. cardinalis* which are on the border-line of winter hardiness. These should be over-wintered as rooted cuttings in a frame as a precaution against root-kill of the parent stock, short pieces of stem being rooted during late summer. However, it is during early spring that most moisture-loving plants are increased from stem cuttings, ideally as growth is just pushing through the soil. Succulent shoots no more than 10 cm (4 in) long, in most cases preferably slightly less, should be removed with a sharp knife. Be sure that each cutting is solid in section, for hollow shoots rarely root.

Having taken the cuttings, trim off any lower leaves that are likely to touch the rooting medium and cause decay. These would also continue to transpire and perhaps cause excessive loss of moisture and wilting. A detached cutting

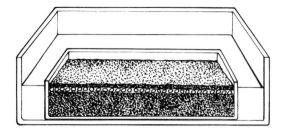

Fig. 7 Seeds of marginal plants should be sown in a good, clean heavy loam and then stood in an outer container filled with water to the level of the compost.

needs an even balance between stem and foliage. Usually after removing the lower leaves it is necessary to reduce the overall leaf area that remains. Do not be frightened to cut leaves in half to achieve this. The stem should then be cut at a leaf joint in order to expose the maximum concentration of active cambium cells and thus enhance rooting. When the cut is made at an angle, an even greater potential rooting zone is exposed. Hormone rooting powders or liquids are invaluable aids to propagation as they encourage the initiation of root-forming cells and at the same time provide a degree of protection from fungal infections. However, be sure that the preparation that you use is fresh, for these products have a limited shelf life.

Once the end of the cutting has been dipped in the hormone preparation it can be inserted in the rooting medium. The choice of medium is wide, but a mixture of equal parts sedge peat and coarse sand or sedge peat and perlite has proved to be very satisfactory for most moisture-loving subjects. Shallow pans are the most useful containers to use. Nobody has discovered the reason, but cuttings of all garden plants seem to root better when inserted around the edge of a pot or pan (Fig. 8.) A moist atmosphere is desirable and this can be provided by inverting a large jar or plastic bag over the pan, although condensation must be removed daily to prevent it dripping on the cuttings and starting decay.

Rooting times vary according to the variety, but once the tip of the cuttings show signs of growth, they must be removed and potted. It is preferable to pot cuttings as soon as they produce roots. Allowing their roots to become entangled in one another leads to possible losses when they are lifted and potted. At this stage the roots are extremely brittle and easily broken.

Pot up rooted cuttings individually in small pots. As they do not have a rootball, great care needs to be taken to see that a pot of sufficient size is used to

(a)   (b)

Fig. 8 Short, non-flowering pieces of stem make excellent cuttings. They root freely in a pan of very wet mud.

accommodate the existing root system, and is in keeping with the aerial parts of the plant. One of the commonest errors in potting young rooted cuttings for the first time is to put them into too large a pot, with the idea that they will not require repotting again. This is a grave mistake, for what usually happens is that the large body of compost around each plant becomes very wet and stale. Even though the plants are moisture-lovers, their delicate young roots come into contact with this and then struggle or die back. When placed in a pot each plant should be held firmly and the compost gently poured around the roots. The young plant should be at the same level in the compost as it was in the pan in which it was rooted. Do not firm the compost down, even if using a soil-based kind, but allow the first watering to settle it.

RAISING MOISTURE-LOVING PLANTS FROM ROOT CUTTINGS

Root cuttings can also be taken of a number of moisture-loving plants, especially the drumstick and candelabra primulas (Fig. 9). Root cuttings are removed from plants that are lifted during the dormant winter period. The best roots are those filled with the vigour of youth which are substantial enough to exist on their own, without drying out, yet are no thicker than a pencil. If this kind of material is cut into sections 2 cm (1 in) or so long, laid horizontally in trays of good potting compost and placed in a cold frame, young plants will be in evidence by late spring. These can then be lifted and treated as seedlings and be potted individually in small pots for planting out the following winter.

RAISING WOODY MOISTURE-LOVING PLANTS FROM CUTTINGS

Although there are few woody moisture lovers that can be accommodated in the modern garden, those like the coloured-stemmed *Salix* and *Cornus* which are regularly stooled are invaluable for providing winter structure, and co-incidentally by their mode of cultivation, cuttings too. These are known as hardwood cuttings. Ideally such cuttings should be taken during the autumn or early winter, but if prunings are depended upon, reasonable success can be obtained in early spring.

When selecting suitable cutting material avoid any shoots that are thin and likely to dry out before rooting, but also any that are thicker than a pencil, as these are likely to be of wood that is too old to root easily. Trim the cuttings to a leaf joint, which during winter is easily recognizable as any point at which there is a dormant bud. Then push them into a well-prepared soil up to about half their length. Some gardeners take out a trench and put sand in the bottom before lining the cuttings out and backfilling. This is unnecessary with either *Salix* or *Cornus* as both root freely when merely pushed into the soil. Cuttings inserted during the autumn will be well rooted by the spring, but those taken during the spring should remain undisturbed until the autumn.

RAISING MARGINAL PLANTS FROM DIVISION AND CUTTINGS

Many marginal plants have a creeping rootstock which can be readily divided. Providing that a piece of root has a strong shoot attached to it, it will usually grow away quickly if planted in very wet conditions. Spring is the best time to do this, just as the plants are coming into growth.

Some marginal plants are clump-forming rather than spreading. These merely require breaking up with a hand fork, the outer portions being used for replanting, as these are much more vigorous than the woody inner portions (Fig. 10). (The same, indeed, applies to many other moisture-loving perennials.)

Creeping marginal plants, like the bog bean (*Menyanthes trifoliata*), and bog arum (*Calla palustris*), are easily increased by the division of their scrambling rhizomes. Bog bean is merely chopped into small sections of stem, each with a latent bud and preferably a vestige of root attached, and then planted in plastic seed trays filled with wet soil until established and sprouting. Bog arum can be increased the same way, but dormant buds that arise along the rhizome can be detached readily and planted out independent of the old stem.

A similar process applies to the flowering rush, *Butomus umbellatus*. Its tiny bulbils appear in the axils of the leaves where they arise from the hard woody

Fig. 9 Some primulas, like *P. denticulata*, can be increased from root cuttings. Remove thick, healthy pieces of root and lay flat on gritty compost. Cover lightly with similar compost, keep warm and moist.

rootstock. If planted in trays of wet compost they rapidly turn into healthy young plants.

Some creeping aquatics are better increased from stem cuttings taken during the spring when the shoots are about 8 cm (3 in) long. These include the water mint, *Mentha aquatica* and brooklime, *Veronica beccabunga*.

RAISING MOISTURE-LOVING FERNS

While the majority of hardy ferns, moisture-loving or not, can be successfully increased by division, the process is very slow. The royal fern, *Osmunda regalis*, for example, may only yield a single division every three or four years, whereas reproduction from spore will produce dozens of plants very quickly.

Growing ferns from spores is not a difficult proposition. It is important to realize, though, that the fern spores are not the exact equivalent of a flowering plant's seed and therefore require slightly different treatment from conventional seeds. In fact it might be said that the spores of a fern are more or less equivalent to the pollen of a flowering plant. While spores can be purchased from the

Fig. 10 Divide old, overgrown clumps of primulas by digging up and dividing into smaller clumps with a handfork. Discard exhausted pieces and replant strong young ones.

seedsman, the degree of success achieved is variable so it is better to gather fresh spores wherever possible. With most ferns these are borne on the undersides of the frond, although occasionally they occur in dense plume-like terminal clusters from the centre of the plant. When ripe the spores are cast on to the wind and it is at this time that they should be collected. The easiest method is to enclose the fertile fronds in a large paper bag, breaking off the frond stalks and upturning both the fronds and bag. Given a vigorous shaking, the spores will detach themselves and fall to the bottom of the bag.

The spores of most species benefit from being sown immediately after collection, especially those from the royal ferns as they contain a small amount of highly perishable chlorophyll which renders then viable for just a few days. Raising the spores need not be complicated. The simplest method uses sterilized clay pans. These are filled with a compost consisting of approximately three parts by volume of sedge peat, one part loam and a dusting of crushed charcoal to keep the mixture sweet. The whole surface area of the pan is then covered with a layer of finely crushed brick dust and the spores sown on this in the same way as one might sow fine seed like that of lobelia or begonia. A small square of glass is then placed over the top of the pan which is stood in a saucer of water in a warm, partially shaded position.

It depends upon the species of variety being grown, but about three weeks after sowing a green mossy growth will begin to smother the surface of the pan. This consists of thousands of little scale-like growths called prothalli which have both male and female elements. Under close humid conditions these elements unite to form embryos which in turn germinate and produce young fern plants. As soon as the first fronds of these tiny ferns are recognizable, the glass should be removed to allow for the free passage of air and to reduce the incidence of damping off disease.

When the young plantlets are large enough to handle they can be lifted in little clumps, the individual baby ferns teased out, and then planted in trays of a regular potting compost.

CHAPTER 8

PESTS AND DISEASES

Fortunately, the grower of moisture-loving and bog plants has very few pests and diseases to contend with. **Slugs** and **snails** often make themselves a nuisance, especially on hostas, ligularias and other succulent plants, usually in early spring just as they are pushing through the soil. But for the most part, the wet bog area escapes their attentions as they are essentially creatures of damp rather than very wet patches. Much can be done to minimize their activities by denying them cover. Good garden hygiene, particularly the removal of dead foliage and other plant debris does much to dissuade the activities of these pests. Once you have them, however, action has to be taken and either pelleted or liquid slug and snail killers administered. These are very much safer than previously, some not killing the creatures, but disrupting their reproductive system.

Water lily aphis are also likely to make themselves a nuisance. They are not specific to water lilies, but infest all manner of succulent aquatic plants, being especially fond of *Butomus* and *Sagittaria*. They look rather like black bean aphis on broad beans, but have a totally different life cycle. It is by disrupting this that the gardener has the best opportunity of beating this pest, for in most circumstances the aphis are not only on the waterside plants, but in the pool itself and therefore cannot be easily sprayed for fear of killing fish and other inhabitants. Similarly, spraying waterside plants can be hazardous as the spray may drift into the water. Additionally, most waterside plants have glossy or waxy foliage from which water is repelled and so it is quite difficult to get a systemic insecticide to stick and become absorbed into the plant's sap stream.

The key to the control of this pest is to spray it during the winter when it has migrated to its overwintering hosts. These are plum and cherry trees, both culinary and ornamental. The aphis over-winter as eggs in the fissures of the bark. A routine spray with an ovicide such as DNOC tar oil wash when the trees are completely dormant will kill the eggs and break the life cycle. It will also destroy a number of overwintering pests which will attack the trees themselves the following season. While this is very effective for the pests lingering in plum and cherry trees in your garden, it does not solve the problem of neighbouring trees that are perhaps unsprayed, so vigilance is needed during the summer as the pests are likely to migrate considerable distances in search of a summer host. Do not be disheartened by this prospect though, for attending to their winter base near at hand will have a significant impact upon the presence of the pests, especially during late spring and early summer.

Other **aphis** attack various moisture-loving plants from time to time, but rarely the true marginal plants, which seem to suffer only the attentions of the water lily aphis. Other aphis are wide and varied in their habits, some only feeding on plants of a particular family or genus, while others are not discerning at all. When aphis are seen it is important to take action immediately. Almost all moisture-loving plants accept systemic insecticides and absorb them without run-off; none is damaged at all by the active ingredient, which is usually dimeothate. This is taken into the sap stream and so spreads throughout the plant. Any aphis that pierces the plant tissue and imbibes the sap is immediately poisoned. This inoculation of the plant persists for about three weeks and so regular spraying is essential if the level of insecticide within the plant is to be maintained.

Systemic insecticides are only fully effective on sucking insects, so a different regime has to be organised for the control of **caterpillars**. There are no major caterpillar pests of waterside plants, but occasionally severe damage can be caused by moth larvae that are specific to one genus or family of plants. These infestations rarely happen, but when they do they can be devastating if immediate action is not taken. Ligularias are favourites for attack, but there are caterpillars that will have a go at *Astilbe* and *Filipendula* as well as *Mimulus*, and *Salix* and *Cornus* are by no means immune either. Chewing insects like this can really only be controlled with a contact killer. Derris dust or rotenone is a natural plant derivative that is effective if applied regularly and is not residual in the soil. The best, though, is HCH dust, but great caution should be taken in its application for it is residual in the soil and can leach into a nearby pool or watercourse. Its use should be greatly restricted and only contemplated if there is no prospect of it entering open water.

Where waterside plants, particularly marginal subjects, grow right in the water they are often attacked by caddis fly larvae. These live in little shelters constructed from all kinds of pond or stream debris and with such protection safely feed on aquatic foliage beneath or resting on the water. There is no real control, for apart from being sturdily built, their structures are also well camouflaged. Fortunately fish consider caddis fly larvae a delicacy and providing the water feature is adequately stocked there should rarely be a problem.

False leaf-mining midge sometimes makes an appearance and when it does the effect can be devastating. The tiny larvae attack the floating foliage of any marginal aquatics, eating a narrow tracery of lines all over the surface. These usually remain unnoticed until the damaged parts become infected and the entire leaf rots and collapses. Forcible spraying of the foliage immediately damage is noticed will control the pest, but by this time the foliage is unlikely to recover.

Fungal diseases do attack waterside and bog garden plants from time to time. Most manifest themselves as a white, sometimes mealy, mildew–like growth. *Filipendula* often succumbs, but control is not difficult. A systemic fungicide in which the active ingredient is benomyl will do the job. It functions within the plant in exactly the same way as a systemic insecticide and while it is inactivated when it falls on the soil, as with a systemic insecticide it is unwise to spray in any area where drift may affect open water.

INDEX